SMALLMOUTH

SMALLMOUTH

Modern Fly-Fishing Methods, Tactics, and Techniques

Dave Karczynski & Tim Landwehr

STACKPOLE
BOOKS

Guilford, Connecticut

Published by Stackpole Books
An imprint of Globe Pequot
Trade Division of The Rowman & Littlefield Publishing Group, Inc.
4501 Forbes Boulevard, Suite 200, Lanham, Maryland 20706
www.rowman.com

Distributed by
NATIONAL BOOK NETWORK
800-462-6420

British Library Cataloguing in Publication Information Available

Library of Congress Cataloging-in-Publication Data Available

ISBN 978-0-8117-1559-1 (paperback)
ISBN 978-0-8117-6597-8 (e-book)

Contents

Acknowledgments

Dave's Acknowledgments

I'd like to thank everyone I've ever shared a boat or beat of river with, first and foremost my parents and my brothers. A special thanks goes out to my uncle, Tony Labeots, one of the fishiest people ever to ply the rivers and bayous of northern Wisconsin. Lastly, I want to express my deep gratitude to all those who contributed insight and images to this book. Their enthusiasm and generosity tells me that, at least within the realm of the smallmouth bass, all is well and only getting better.

Tim's Acknowledgments

I have been fortunate to have had the opportunity to learn this sport and spend time on the water with so many people. I can't thank all my clients enough for the years we have spent in the boat together learning and laughing. Friends that freely shared information, fly patterns, and even that secret spot on occasion. Without these friends and mentors, I could not have come this far.

Thank you to all of my guides who tirelessly row the boat every day on the hunt for river smallmouth. This book would not be possible without their knowledge and vast experience. Guide camp is a constant think tank each summer, and the guys that guide for Tight Lines are the best in the business. They are like brothers to me, and I could not be more proud to be on their team. They have freely shared all they have to offer with us to bring you this book.

I must thank my good friend Dave De Keyser. Dave was with me on the first float trip on the river and convinced me that people would book guide trips for smallmouth bass. At that time trout had dominated the fly-fishing scene, and without his encouragement our guide business would never have happened.

Thanks to my good friends Dave and Emily Whitlock for encouraging me and pushing us to learn as much as possible about the smallmouth bass. Dave and Emily's words and open-mindedness pushed me to step out of the norm and learn techniques not yet used for smallmouth bass.

Much appreciation to my family. My mom and dad, brother Tom, and sister Jean for encouraging me and always supporting my crazy fishing lifestyle. These people have shaped who I am and have always been there for me regardless of how ridiculous my ideas were.

And finally, thanks to my amazing wife, Sarah, and my two kids and fishing partners, Noah and Avery. Sarah has allowed me to follow my dream of having a fly shop, to travel the world for exotic species, and to continue my guiding career. Having her love and support through this crazy journey has made all of this possible. To her I owe everything.

Foreword

I caught my first smallmouth bass on a fly when I was just twelve years old. I was standing in a beautiful, clear, spring-fed stream in the lovely, northeastern Oklahoma Ozarks. That experience started a seventy-year love affair with these wonderful, red-eyed, tiger-striped torpedoes. To this day they are still my most favorite fish to catch on a fly. Over the years I have sought these hard-fighting fish in many, many waters across North America and have never been disappointed.

Often these encounters have come about as a result of my professional fly-fishing travel activities for fly-fishing clubs, fly shops, and expos. In fact, Emily and I were engaged in just such activities when we first visited Tim Landwehr's fly shop—Tight Lines—in De Pere, Wisconsin. Little did I suspect that it would be so significant in enhancing my life's devotion and pleasure for smallmouth!

After our shop appearance Tim asked if we'd like to spend part of the next day fly fishing with him on his local waters—trout or bass, our choice. We eagerly accepted his invitation, and when we chose the smallmouth river his eyed suddenly widened and a big smile of approval and delight came over his face. "Good choice! I'll float you down my favorite river—the smallmouth are outta-sight there!"

And they were! What a fantastic experience—drifting down this incredibly beautiful river with smallmouth soul mates, Tim and Emily. There seemed to be a big, full-bodied smallmouth in every spot that we cast our poppers, crayfish, and streamers. Emily and I were in heaven! It was very obvious that this clean-cut, handsome young man "got it" when it came to knowing, respecting, and loving smallmouth and how special they are. Many times since that afternoon, we have joined Tim and his guides, building a rich base of knowledge of fly fishing for smallmouth bass. After several thousand trips down most of the upper Midwest's prime smallmouth rivers, Tim and his brilliant staff have pooled their extensive experience and understanding with that of

---

Facing: Big, small, or somewhere in between, few fish have accounted for more smiles than the smallmouth bass. Here author and educator Dave Whitlock takes a topwater fish from a shallow riffle. Riffles add oxygen to a river system and nourish many populations of aquatic insects, which in turn nourish bass as they grow in size and move up the food chain. DAVE WHITLOCK

their clients, fishery biologists, and the published works of other smallmouth addicts like myself and created this book, a book that is truly a definitive smallmouth treatise that elevates smallmouth to the prestige they deserve and, in my opinion, a book destined to become a classic.

When I began to review this manuscript, my expectations were pretty high, but just a couple of chapters into it I realized that this was no ordinary manuscript. It has actually exceeded my expectations and has significantly enhanced my seventy years of fly-fishing experience for these wonderful creatures. With each new chapter and topic, I found myself thinking how very fortunate readers of this book will be. Tim, Dave, and their team masterfully use many true-experience anecdotes to emphasize smallmouth facts and theories, clarify the text, and entertain us. Add to this the photos and diagrams that are superbly rendered to fully visualize the text.

Truly this book is a master golden key to unlock and open the world of smallmouth at the highest level of fly-fishing literature. Tim and Dave set the bar at its highest mark to show their ultimate respect and admiration for smallmouth by never killing smallmouth to photograph or mount. They also

Wet-wading for smallmouth provides heat relief for anglers, but that's not all. Solar heat activates a variety of winged food items, such as dragonflies. Warm weather also increases a bass's metabolism. Put the two together and what do you get? Comfortable fishing and steady topwater action, as Emily Whitlock demonstrates with this healthy adult smallmouth. DAVE WHITLOCK

For boat angling, a long-handled net with a wide, deep basket is an essential tool of the trade. Smallmouth are notorious jumpers and hook-throwers, so the sooner you can get them into the net, the better. A good net also reduces the amount of time a fish needs to be played before landing. Along with tackle properly fitted to the fish, appropriate landing tools ensure that fish are released with a minimum of lactic acid buildup, which in high doses can be toxic. DAVE WHITLOCK

---

do not fish to beds or spawners. Their guiding equipment is the best—always clean and in perfect working order—as are the guides.

Smallmouth have earned my love by always being relentlessly strong, nearly tireless fighters that use every square inch of water, structure, and even air to defeat us. They're like Jack Russells—even the small ones don't know they are small. And, despite our abuses of their environments, climate change, and increasing angling pressure, they are on the increase. Unfortunately many other species, because of these same reasons, are declining and must be stocked to keep up populations. The majority of trout in the United States are stocked, while 99 percent of smallmouth are indigenous or introduced, self-reproducing fish. Just take a minute to make eye contact with the red-eyed, wild glare of the next smallmouth you catch and you'll get the message. Just one more thing: I must admit that I've met with defeat from large smallmouth more than any other species of fish I've hooked fly fishing.

There's no doubt in my mind that Tim and Dave's book will initiate a new era for smallmouth bass and smallmouth bass fly fishers.

Dave Whitlock

CHAPTER 1

Introduction

The other day Dave was preparing for a smallmouth trip when a friend from the other side of the Atlantic shot him a message.

"What are you up to?"

"Getting ready to hit the water."

"For what?"

"Smallmouth bass."

Even though Dave's friend was an avid angler, being a European he had no idea what a smallmouth was. "Can you describe it for me?" he asked. Dave thought long and hard and spent several minutes describing the fish to the best of his ability.

"So, a smallmouth is like a pike," his friend said.

Anglers Ben Lubchansky (left) and Kyle Zempel (right) are halfway to a double-header on the Wisconsin River. Note the position of Kyle's line hand—so far from his reel it's almost behind him. The key to staying stuck to a freshly hooked bass is to perform several long strips that take your hand past your waist. Short strips will simply not gather enough line to keep up with a stuck fish that decides to charge the boat. ERIC CHRISTENSEN

While a big smallmouth may eat a surface bug or even crayfish daintily, all subtlety goes out the window when the fight begins. By tucking the fighting butt of his rod against his torso, this angler is able to keep leverage on the fish during the last few crucial moments of the fight. NATE SIPPLE

"Not really," Dave explained. "They only really grow to four or five pounds, which is probably good because if they grew to twenty or thirty pounds no one would ever land one. They're also a structure-oriented fish, thriving in current and feeding on seams."

"Ah, so it's like a trout."

"No again. Smallmouth are definitely more opportunistic than selective. And, furthermore, a bass's reasons for eating and refusing flies are a good deal different from a brown trout's."

This comparison of species went on for some time, until they'd exhausted the game fish of Europe. Dave thought his friend was frustrated by having nothing in his home waters to compare to the smallmouth bass. But his friend's reaction was very different.

"It sounds like the perfect fish for anglers," he said.

Dave smiled and quoted Dr. James Henshall, the bass's first unapologetic devotee: "Pound for pound and inch for inch it's the gamest fish that swims."

This book is built on the belief that the smallmouth bass is, indeed, a perfect fish for anglers, in all the ways Dave's friend observed and so many more. First off, it occupies a variety of riparian environments, north and south, east and west, rural and urban. This accessibility means a lot of current and potential fly anglers live near quality smallmouth water.

Second, the smallmouth is a fish whose arrow of fortune is pointing decidedly upward. Habitat improvement and an embrace of ethical fishing practices that leave spawning fish to reproduce in peace have contributed to some fantastic smallmouth conditions in rivers across the country.

Third, and perhaps most interestingly, the practice of smallmouth fishing makes use of the widest possible set of fly-fishing tools and skills. To be a true master of the sport, you'll need to acquire the complete fly-fishing tool kit: from the delicate presentation casts of dry-fly trout fishing to the vision, accuracy, and adjustment of hunting the saltwater flats—and everything in between. It's this fact that makes smallmouth fishing such an exciting game, and it's also this fact that makes this such a necessary book.

How This Book Came About

It's impossible to tell the story of this book without telling the story of Tight Lines Fly Shop. In 2001 Tim quit his job at a bank in De Pere, Wisconsin, and opened a fly shop, very much against the warnings (and a few failed interventions) of friends and family. It was, like most any fly shop in the country at that time, totally trout oriented, even though Tim and his fishing partners fished mostly for smallmouth when they had a day to themselves. And Tim's shop might still be that way to this day—serving up trout paraphernalia to customers while smallmouth fishing during private time—if not for one very particular day on the water.

"I was just sitting around when I got a call from a good friend, a pure trout angler," Tim explained. "He wanted to go fishing—trout fishing of course. But I wanted to do something different that day. The truth is, I loved smallmouth but was afraid to talk about it. It was like this dirty secret. But that day, talking to my friend on the phone, I decided I was tired of keeping it hidden: I knew we had this amazing fishery and that smallmouth were an amazing fish. But I also knew my friend was a pure trout guy, at a time when fly fishing was 99.9 percent pure trout guys. But for some reason I decided to take the risk."

Tim's friend didn't like the idea at first. "Tell me again why we're going smallmouth fishing?" he asked as they backed the boat into the river. But he went along with the plan, tying on a large frog-imitating popper. They'd only gotten a few yards downstream of the launch when an eighteen-inch fish came up, inhaled the bug, and proceeded to go airborne five times before coming to hand.

The day turned out to be one of the most epic days of topwater fishing ever. Tim watched his friend catch fish after fish. By the end of the day, Tim's

Epic days are not only for the middle of summer. Here Tim Landwehr hoists two large pre-spawn bass caught within seconds of each other. Find one cold-water bass and you have likely found many more. Savvy anglers will drop anchor and explore the lie with a variety of presentation techniques and angles before moving on. NATE SIPPLE

trout-angler friend turned to him and said, "This is the best day of fishing I've ever had in my entire life."

Tim, for his part, was surprised. In his best-case scenario, he was simply hoping his trout-centric friend wouldn't hate him for being forced to fish smallmouth. He certainly didn't expect the kind of enthusiasm he was now seeing. And so Tim looked at him point-blank and asked, "Do you think people would pay to fish smallmouth?"

Fifteen years, thousands of floats, and many more thousands of happy clients later, the answer is a resounding, wall-shaking yes.

The Evolution of Our Principles, Tactics, and Techniques

Early in his smallmouth guiding career, Tim gave a talk to a group of Chicago anglers on tactics and techniques for catching river bass. The title of his talk? "The Green Trout." As you might imagine, in his talk Tim advocated for a trout-centric approach to the bass. Now, fifteen years later, he shakes his head in embarrassment at how little he knew and how wrong he was.

Of course, Tim was not alone in treating the smallmouth bass like a warm-water trout. It was really the only approach anyone had going at the time. In the early days of smallmouth bass fishing, there wasn't much of a template to go off of, and much of the theory and practice of smallmouth fishing came from the trout world. Even progressive smallmouth anglers like Tim and his cousin Bart fished with trout tactics, and not even terribly modern trout tactics either—after all, Kelly Galloup's *Modern Streamers for Trophy Trout* would not come out until well into their guiding program's maturity. So instead of throwing Sex Dungeons, they dead-drifted hellgrammites. Instead of working Murdich Minnows, they fished Woolly Buggers. In between, there was a lot of dry fly fishing—with Adamses. There was also some largemouth bass influence, too, that came in the form of massive hair bugs and whatever else came in those packages of eight flies from the big-box stores.

In addition to the primitive flies and presentations, knowledge of where smallmouth were to be found in a river was also hopelessly simplistic. In those days, smallmouth anglers basically drifted down the middle of the river and threw poppers to the banks. Not a few feet from the bank but right on the bank. Now we know that the bank, or the "first shelf," as we often refer to it in this book, is only one of many smallmouth microhabitats.

And microhabits are not the only thing. We now know so much more about so many aspect of smallmouth life and behavior.

Through the proliferation of new smallmouth fly designs and lines, new worlds of understanding have emerged. From early innovators like Dave Whitlock, Lefty Kreh, and Bob Clouser to modern guys like Blane Chocklett, Mike Schultz, and the authors of this book, fly anglers have come a tremendously long way in understanding the bass. Over the years we've looked far outside the box to develop new approaches. We've looked to and learned from gear anglers. We've adopted relevant saltwater practices. In doing so, we have advanced light-years in our understanding of how, when, where, and why a bass moves to a fly. We now know that the smallmouth bass is a very particular type of opportunist, with a psychology all its own. And so this book attempts to take all of the discoveries of the past fifteen years in the sprawling tannined

Smallmouth are street brawlers deserving of a respectful release. After doing battle, face a fish upstream into slow-flowing current while supporting its body weight with your hand. Resuscitation may take longer on hotter days, when levels of dissolved oxygen are lower. KYLE ZEMPEL

laboratories of northern Wisconsin and put them into a system that will help anglers at any stage of their fly-fishing practice catch more and bigger bass.

It's true that you can take a simple approach to smallmouth bass fishing and have some success with it. But the true beauty of the sport, and the reason for this book, is that you can be much, much more successful by understanding the finer details of the smallmouth game. No matter where you are in your smallmouth fishing career, there are things you can learn from this book. Just ask Lefty Kreh.

One day Tim had Lefty and Lefty's friend Jim in the boat. Jim was fishing wigglies all day and doing very well. But Lefty refused to give the wiggly a try and spent the day rotating through big poppers, Deceivers, and Half-and-Halfs. The results of his efforts were just a scant few fish. Lefty could not believe that Jim's fly, which looked essentially like a bluegill spider, could possibly work better than a big foam popper. And yet Jim outfished him all through the afternoon.

Toward the end of the day, Tim saw three fish on a sand flat, right on the edge of a weed line. The water was calm and shallow, and even Lefty could see that it was no time for a big fly. "Throw the wiggly," Tim told Jim. The first fish came up, looked at the fly, tipped up on it but then slid back and didn't eat. Tim tied on another wiggly, and this time a second fish came up and performed the same type of lazy refusal. Finally, Tim put on an articulated damselfly patterns and punched that out. The fly slid down over the flat, and without hesitation a nineteen-inch fish came up and sipped it in like a cutthroat. After the fish was landed, Lefty looked at his guide and said, "Timmy, you are one smallmouth bass catching son-of-a-bitch." It was the best compliment Tim had ever gotten in his entire fishing life.

We'll add one last anecdote that demonstrates just how much fun a good day of smallmouth bass fishing can be. One day back in the late 1990s, the Tight Lines crew was hosting a client whose name will go unmentioned here. Suffice it to say he had founded a very successful company and was exceedingly well-to-do, but at the age of eighty-eight he was in such poor health that he required an oxygen tank and a nurse with him at all times—including on the drift boat. Despite these obstacles, his guide was surprised to note that his casting stroke was actually quite decent. Shortly after launching, this elderly client was thick into fish, smiling, laughing, and looking less and less frail by the minute. It was shaping up to be not just a good day but a spectacular one when around noon his nurse leaned over to the rower and whispered, "Are we almost done?"

The rower was confused by the question and shook his head. "Only half done," he said. "We've got four more hours to the takeout."

Controlling your loop at distance is key to being a successful flats angler. In the image below, Tim Landwehr prepares to lay a small baitfish pattern at the back of a shallow flat. By landing the fly softly and twitching it immediately, Tim has a good chance of goading any nearby fish into eating—not fleeing. MICHAEL LESCHISIN

The nurse's face went white. "We don't have four hours of oxygen."

What transpired next was a feat of rowing the likes of which the rivers of the Midwest had never seen. Huffing it to high heaven, the boat made the launch in two hours, where an ambulance was waiting. No sooner had the boat breached the bank than the EMTs were lifting the gasping client out of the boat. Apparently his oxygen requirements had been estimated according to a normal day of living, not one in which smallmouth in the eighteen- to twenty-inch class were slamming bugs on the surface all day long.

In roughly thirty seconds both the client and his nurse were gone, the ambulance raising a plume of dust in the forest.

"Well," Tim said. "I guess that's the last we'll see of him."

Only it wasn't: The next morning he and his nurse were waiting dutifully outside the hotel. By the time the boat launched, it was loaded with so many oxygen tanks it looked like a Jacques Cousteau expedition.

The takeaway? Smallmouth are worth giving it your all.

Meet the Authors

Though Dave and Tim are listed as the primary authors, this book has been very much a team effort. Whenever you hear the word "we," you might think of it as a Greek chorus of smallmouth junkies with tens of thousands of river hours to their credit, on rivers large and small, clear and stained, tricklingly low and frighteningly blown out, their banks sometimes crusted with snow, other times burnt crisp by the August sun.

Writer and photographer **DAVE KARCZYNSKI** is a regular contributor to *Outdoor Life, Fly Rod & Reel, The Drake,* MidCurrent.com, and many other publications. A Robert Traver Award winner and writing instructor at the University of Michigan, Dave's love of words and water is his driving passion. His pursuit of the smallmouth bass goes back to his teenage years, when the discovery of the awesome nature of *Micropterus dolomieu* transformed him from a casual angler into a committed one. He lives in Ann Arbor, Michigan.

Writer and coauthor Dave Karczynski.

DAVE KARCZYNSKI

TIM LANDWEHR owns and operates Tight Lines Fly Shop in De Pere, Wisconsin. Tim has been guiding for smallmouth bass for the majority of his adult life in the cradle of smallmouth civilization: the brawling freestoners of northern Wisconsin. He has been featured on ESPN Outdoors, *Fly Fisherman* magazine, *Gray's Sporting Journal, Catch Magazine,* the *Fly Fishing Film Tour, Badger Sportsman, Eastern Fly Fishing, Sporting Classics,* and has hosted the *Midwest Sportsman* television program. Tim has had the privilege to fish with some of the greats of the sport and has guided fly-fishing legends Dave Whitlock and Lefty Kreh on a number of occasions. Tim's vast knowledge of smallmouth has been earned from thousands of guided trips down his favorite smallmouth rivers. He lives in De Pere, Wisconsin.

Guide, Tight Lines Fly Shop founder, and coauthor Tim Landwehr. NATE SIPPLE

BART LANDWEHR was born and raised in proximity to the best smallmouth water in the world. He grew up with a love of all things outdoors—fishing in particular. After trading in conventional tackle for a fly rod in his teens, Bart immersed himself in the world of fly fishing, and since then he has fished for just about every freshwater species that will eat a fly. His guiding career started in the Rocky Mountains, but his love of rivers and the smallmouth bass ultimately brought him back home to northern Wisconsin. Now heading into his sixteenth season as a smallmouth river guide, Bart has earned a deep understanding of the species from between the oars. He is recognized in the industry as an innovative fly tier, excellent teacher, and all-around fun guy to spend time with on the river. He currently resides in Green Bay, Wisconsin.

Guide Bart Landwehr. MICHAEL LESCHISIN

Guide Nate Sipple. NATE SIPPLE

NATE SIPPLE has just entered his eleventh year of guiding the rivers of northern Wisconsin. He averages 140 days per year on the water in exclusive pursuit of smallmouth bass. All this time and experience has given him a wealth of knowledge that benefits himself and his clients on a daily basis. His deep understanding of the smallmouth as a species gives him absolute confidence in being able to find them in any river environment, any time of year. He lives in Shawano, Wisconsin.

Guide Charlie Piette. NATE SIPPLE

CHARLIE PIETTE is the longtime manager of Tight Lines Fly Fishing Co. in De Pere, Wisconsin. He began his life in the fly industry as a nineteen-year-old college sophomore and never left. More than a dozen years later, he now has a completely unused Masters of Environmental Science and Policy (with associated debt), a drift boat, and a collection of tying materials that would rival many fly shops! Despite widely varied fishing addictions, Charlie is proud to call Wisconsin home. As a guide, he pursues the premier seasonal bounties in the land of beer and cheese: river smallmouth bass and Driftless-area trout. Outside of the guide season, Charlie hosts destination travel in the United States and abroad. When not on the water, he is most likely found at Tight Lines, where he continues to share his enthusiasm for the sport with others by coordinating destination travel and teaching fly-fishing and fly-tying schools. Charlie's fly-tying videos for Tight Line's Fly Shop's YouTube channel have been viewed by more than three hundred thousand anglers.

Also, because smallmouth fishing takes place in a wide variety of different habitats, each with different microclimates and geological eccentricities, we have included a substantial sampling of other voices from yesterday's and today's best *Micropterus* hunters. You'll find their wisdom at the end of the book in the chapter entitled "Other Voices."

Last, we feel it's essential to acknowledge the authors that preceded us. The first true work on fly fishing for bass was the *Book of the Black Bass,* written by James A. Henshall, first published in Cincinnati in 1881 by Robert Clarke & Co. Since that time Harry Murray, Tim Holchslag, Dave Whitlock, Bob Clouser, Lefty Kreh, and others have written fantastic and groundbreaking books on smallmouth. We are indebted to all of these authors and their amazing work.

How to Use This Book

Our philosophy in writing this book has been to encourage anglers to start thinking about their flies not as general foodstuffs, but as presentation technologies. Simply put, different fly designs allow you to cover water at different depths and speeds, and with different actions and profiles. For this reason, we've broken the water column into three meat-and-potato chapters, each dedicated to attacking one portion of the water column, from the top to the middle to the bottom. One happy by-product of this systematic, fly-centric approach is that it will help you become not only a better and more thoughtful smallmouth angler, but a more deliberate and effective angler in general.

There is one other way in which this book differs from other technical fly-fishing books. One regards recommended tackle—rods, reels, lines, and the like. You'll see that instead of lumping it all together in one chapter, we've elected to situate tackle discussions alongside conversations about different column-specific flies and presentations. We like to get as detailed as possible when talking about lines, rods, and riggings, so locating these discussions alongside actual presentation instruction just makes more sense to us.

CHAPTER 2

Rivers and Seasons

The best smallmouth bass water exists in something of a Goldilocks state. Current speed is typically moderate—not as fast as a trout stream but not as slow as a largemouth bass and catfish river. Smallmouth rivers are likewise not too shallow and not too deep, which make them amenable to boat anglers and wading anglers alike. Perhaps best of all, smallmouth rivers are also in the sweet spot in terms of temperature—warm enough to wet-wade through for the bulk of the season but cool enough to provide a blast of refreshment when the thermometer heads north of ninety degrees. The temperate nature of smallmouth rivers means that, for the majority of the season, very little is required in terms of specialty attire: A pair of shorts and some wet-wading shoes will do for gear, with sunblock generally a more useful tool than chest waders—just one more reason smallmouth bass truly are "the angler's fish."

The smallmouth bass's liberal habitat requirements mean you can find excellent smallmouth fishing in a wide variety of areas, from roaring northern

This angler demonstrates the right angle for a topwater hook set: straight up. Strip setting or even setting to the side can result in the fly being pulled out of a fish's partly open mouth. KYLE ZEMPEL

Understanding the way smallmouth bass relate to shelves is essential to successful fishing. Here the drift boat sits on the first shelf as the angler in the rear of the boat swings a baitfish pattern across the second shelf. Focus on the second, deeper shelf when shallow water and bright light conditions make the first shelf too dangerous a hunting ground for smallmouth. NATE SIPPLE

freestoners coursing through canyons of white pine, to pastoral rivers meandering through farm country, to suburban rivers flowing past backyards, patios, and municipal parks.

But geology and human development along the riparian corridor affect not only the scenery of a river but also the river's size, flow, color, and fundamental structure. Some rivers, such as Flambeau, Chippewa, and Menominee of northern Wisconsin, are large, swift, and wide, with plenty of rock ledges and boulder fields. At their clearest, these rivers have the color of weak tea, the product of tannins in the surrounding soil. Other rivers, such as Michigan's Muskegon, Au Sable, and Huron Rivers, feature sand bottoms and clearer water. These differences play key roles in determining how smallmouth in a given river system eat and behave. That said, for the purposes of understanding how to approach smallmouth bass—where to find them, what flies to select and how to present them—the most valuable feature of a given piece of water is the structural orientation of the river corridor.

Throughout this book we'll be thinking about smallmouth rivers (and beats of rivers) as x-axis or y-axis systems. We'll call x-axis water those straighter channels with long primary and secondary shelves running in a line more or less parallel to shore or the path of a boat. As a rule larger rivers tend to have more x-axis water, as do rivers flowing through corridors of hard rock and shale. Y-axis water, on the other hand, are those windier rivers or beats of rivers with curving channels, irregular holes, and wood debris stacked up at river bends. On y-axis water, structure is more likely to fall along a line perpendicular to shore and a boat's path. Smaller rivers and those coursing through softer sediment tend to have more y-axis water than the above-mentioned rivers.

Our focus on structural orientation is particularly important given the fly-focused nature of this book. Simply put, an x-axis or y-axis river will affect presentation recommendations. To provide a basic, if slightly exaggerated, illustration, the below diagram demonstrates two different rivers. With fish in the second image relating to x-axis structure, the most effective means of presentation might involve a fly that can be drifted with the current along the primary or secondary shelf; a surface fly dead-drifted from a moving drift boat would be the quintessential x-axis presentation. The first image, however, shows us a different situation. Here, a dead-drift along a shelf becomes inefficient, impractical, and, because of the exposed timber, impossible. Here, a baitfish pattern fished aggressively back to the boat would represent the quintessential y-axis presentation. Recognizing the major structural features of your river will help you plan a day's float or wade and approach water most systematically and efficiently.

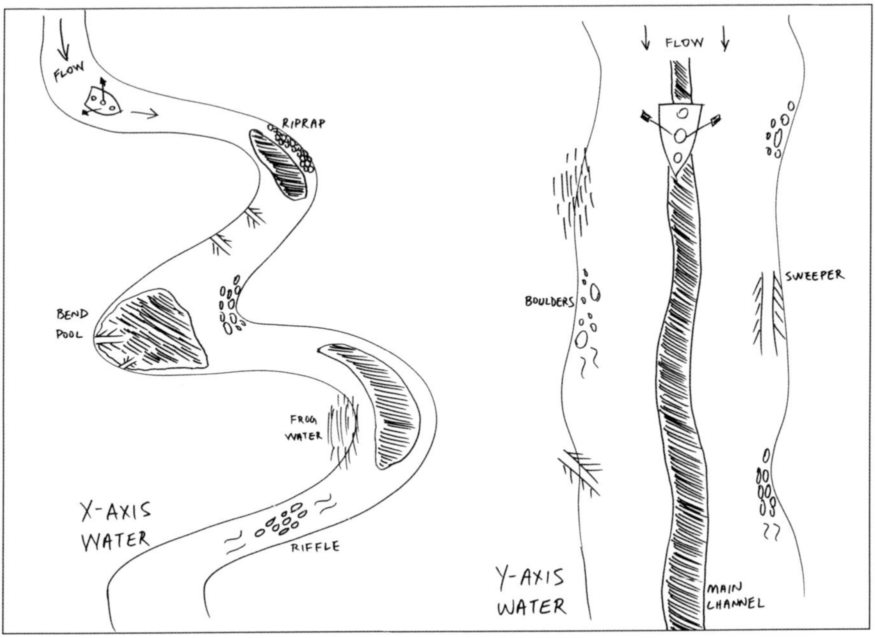

The beat of water on the left is classic y-axis water. With irregular holes and irregular obstructions, presentations like baitfish patterns that move steadily back to the boat are the best bet. The beat of water on the right is classic x-axis water. The most efficient presentations will both with those flies that can be dead-drifted, wafted with the current, or bumped downstream along the bottom. DAVE KARCZYNSKI

Bass Movement Throughout the Seasons

With minor variations between different types of watersheds, the general movement of smallmouth bass throughout the year is one of cold-water compression and warm-water expansion. Depending on your river system, smallmouth might move anywhere from a few hundred yards to a few dozen miles between winter and summer habitat. Let's look a little more specifically at how smallmouth respond to changes in water temperatures and water flows throughout the year.

PRE-SPAWN

It's true that the odd smallmouth bass is caught by walleye anglers very early and very late in the season when water temperatures are in the thirties. However, it's typically not until water temperatures move into the upper forties that bass can be effectively presented to with a fly and fly rod. And while bass can be targeted at that time, it's usually not until water temperatures get closer to the fifty-degree mark that bass metabolism revs up enough to make for consistent quality fishing with a fly rod.

If you live in a state with a closed bass season, the activity of bass on the opener will vary by year: Sometimes fish will be very active prior to the start of the season and you can hit the ground running. Other times the season will begin with snow on the banks, cold temperatures, and very lethargic fish. Whatever the case, it's important to remember that our human concept of a fishing "season" doesn't always correlate with a bass's. A preternaturally warm week of weather in March may make for good days of fishing far ahead of schedule. Likewise, a patch of belated winter weather in May could put a serious damper on your first serious smallmouth outing of the year.

In the early season, water temperature is far and away the most important factor for smallmouth success, and it can be worth thinking about how to put yourself on the warmest water possible. Begin by asking yourself this: What part of a given river system should I fish?

Any trout angler knows that rivers typically gain temperature the farther they get from their headwaters. Downstream stretches tend to be naturally warmer. The current is slower and the substrate is siltier, creating more particulate matter in the water to absorb the sun's energy. But there are other factors to take into consideration as well. One is the presence and location of major ice buildup on your watershed. In the smallmouth bass's northernmost range, ice can remain on backwaters, feeder lakes, and dam impoundments

High spring water and cool temps reward anglers who understand the thermal patterns of their river system. This fish came from the mouth of a shallow tributary that gained solar heat as it coursed through sun-drenched farmland. In the early season, even a difference of a few degrees can have a huge impact on fish behavior and aggression. HEIDI OBERSTADT

well into the fishing season. Early season smallmouth anglers should stay away from heavy concentrations of ice, which will leech cold water into the system even (and especially) on warmer days.

Tributaries are another important factor in our hunt for the warmest possible early season water. The temperatures of tributaries can vary a good deal, so make a point to learn how each inflow into your system compares to the temperature of the main branch. We recommend doing this twice a year, once in the early season and once again midsummer, since feeder creeks may not always provide a temperature advantage. A thermally regulated spring-fed feeder creek might be a fish magnet in the spring when the main river is just waking up, but if it stays temperate year-round, in July it might just become a too-cool smallmouth desert. The moral of the story is to get to know the temperatures on the tributaries of the river system you fish. Some will hold fish year-round, while others will primarily be important during early and late in the season.

Another thing to pay attention to is sunlight. At any given moment one side of the river is receiving more sunlight than the other, and there will be a resulting bump in temperature there. For that reason, we advocate focusing

Preferred early season fly colors will vary according to your watershed and its fishing pressure and available prey items. Devote some time in the early season to experimenting with unnatural vs. natural colors, as well as different flash quantities. No two river systems are alike, and you may be surprised by how fish preferences vary. LUKE KAVAJECZ

your attention on the sunny side of the bank, especially on larger rivers where working both sides of the boat might be difficult. The sunny side of the river will always be a degree or two warmer than the other side, and in the early season that single degree can make a huge difference on fish activity.

The last temperature-related factor to take into consideration early and late in the year is time of day. Spring and fall are not the time to fish extra early or extra late. On any given day a river's temperature rises, but it's during the early part of the season that a rise in temperatures can make or break an outing. For that reason you should definitely prioritize the warmest part of the day—those hours between noon and four o'clock in the afternoon. Spring fishing is often characterized by a flurry of fish activity during peak temps, so you definitely want to be in position to fish quality water when that bite window opens up.

It's often said that in the early part of the year, 95 percent of the fish are in 5 percent of the water. Whether the ratio is 90:10 or 85:15, the fact of the matter is that fish are not spread out throughout the system in the same way they'll be in just a few more weeks' time. This means that it's all too easy for an uninformed angler to make a day's worth of quality presentations to water that simply does not hold bass. If you're fishing for early season bass the same way you fish for summer bass, you're doing it wrong. You need a totally different mind-set for early season fish. As Tim likes to say, "In the summer I fish all the spots I'd never touch in the spring. And in the spring I fish all the spots I never touch in the summer."

But what exactly is "quality early season water" anyways? There are two basic qualities that need to be present in early season smallmouth water: depth and softness. Let's start by talking about that softness. Soft, slow current is where smallmouth bass can stage in preparation for spring without expending too much energy. We are basically looking for the softest water we can find that still has some proximity to the main flow of the river. And while slow is good, "not moving" can be even better. Think coves, the slowest parts of larger eddy systems, pools behind larger deadfalls or wingdams, railroad trestles, bridge crossings, and, of course, dams.

But soft water alone does not make for good early season holding water. It also needs to be deep. How deep? That depends on your river. Early season water should be a good deal deeper than what is average for your river, and the best early season holding water will be a deeper hole on a beat of river with plenty of other deeper holes. On some watersheds, four to five feet may suffice. On others, fish will hold at ten to twelve feet (once we get much deeper than fifteen feet, these fish become difficult if not impossible to apprehend with a fly rod).

Once you find these early season fish, *stop moving and stay on those fish.* Where there's one, there's likely a lot more, and you may struggle to find fish

Dave Karczynski demonstrates the right way to fish a sinking line: rod tip pointed at where the fly line enters the water, eyes downstream to scope out the placement of the next cast. TOM HAZELTON

later in the day. A perfect example of the pitfalls of abandoning known players happened just last year while we were doing scouting for the imminent guide season. With the season's first clients arriving in just a few days, it was time to see what the fish were up to. Tim and Nate launched below a dam on one of our regular beats. Tim was on the oars and rowed the boat to the softer water below the dam. With water temperatures hovering at just below forty-five degrees and no chance of an afternoon bump, presentations needed to be slow and right in the fish's face to get any response from a lethargic bass. Nate began fishing a long untapered leader to get his dredger down as deep as he could. Almost immediately he was fast into a giant pre-spawn female—and the first fish of the season was in the boat. We plucked big fish off the bottom for the next two hours, all within sight of the dam. On a six-mile float that typically takes all day, we landed literally dozens of big-river smallmouth within three hundred yards of the launch. As soon as we pushed down from the dam, however, our prospects changed dramatically, and we went fishless for the next five hours on the river. Had we skipped the dam water and fished like it was midsummer, we would have put no fish in the boat instead of dozens.

The moral of the story? Don't leave smallmouth to find smallmouth before the water temperature reaches fifty degrees—usually the point at which bass begin spreading to other microhabitats throughout the system.

THE SPAWN AND POST-SPAWN

As the water warms and starts to approach sixty degrees, bass begin to stage for the spawn. On larger rivers that lack suitable spawning habitat (silty bottoms, developed shoreline, or heavy boat traffic), it's at this time of year that fish may enter tributaries with habitat more amenable to procreation. Following fish from the tributary mouths upstream with the warming water can be key to finding pre-spawn fish on the move. And move they can. The longest smallmouth migration ever recorded was seventy miles—a fair amount of traveling for a fish not considered to be migratory in nature. On those river systems where longer-distance migration is common, water levels will play a factor in determining whether smallmouth will return to the main river after spawning or remain in the tributaries through the summer. Higher than normal flows may result in smallmouth spending all summer in tributaries before returning to bigger water in the fall. Conversely, during years of relatively low water, smallmouth may decamp for more spacious downriver environs shortly after spawning is conducted.

Whether you're following fish into the tributaries or sticking to the main branch of a classic smallmouth river, it's important to remember that not all smallmouth spawn at the same time. Some fish spawn early, while others spawn late—it's a matter of individual preference and genetic inclination.

There's nothing sporting about targeting a smallmouth bass on its bed. It only takes a minute for a bass's nest to be raided by a variety of egg-loving creatures. Leave bedded bass to spawn in peace by focusing your efforts on the second shelf and mid-river seams. NATE SIPPLE

These tendencies mean that, at any given day during spawning season, you may encounter fish in two or even three stages of their seasonal progression, from pre-spawn to post. It's important to note that fish in different stages will not be found side by side—good news for the ethical angler trying to avoid casting to spawning fish. They will use the river differently and have a different pattern of, and rationale for, coming to the fly.

The easiest way to identify the spawn is by either seeing fish on beds or seeing empty beds (since your approach may have sent fish scurrying). That said, smallmouth beds in rivers can be more difficult to see than, say, largemouth beds in a lake. Cover and structure is paramount to good spawning habitat; very rarely do we see a smallmouth bed just sitting in the open without some type of overhead or submerged structure. Low-hanging limbs, spaces between sunken logs, small coves, or even the area under a dock all provide the necessary habitat for spawning smallmouth.

When you see smallmouth beds, it's best to move along. In the same way that we advocate for the protection of trout and salmon on redds, we strongly discourage the targeting of bass on spawning beds. Simply put, it's just not sporting or fun. Just how unfair fishing to spawning bass is can be revealed by the following anecdote. An angler at the shop was recounting a day of fishing the shallow bays of Lake Michigan at a time when these fish would most certainly have been guarding their beds. He remarked loudly about how amazed he was that he caught the same fish three times over the course of the same day: Every time he put his fly in the vicinity of this bass, the fish leisurely swam over and picked it up. After listening to him talk a bit more, it became clear that he wasn't an unsporting angler, just an ill-informed one. When he learned that the bass were simply trying to keep their nests clean and free of predators that might be looking for a quick and easy meal of eggs, he suddenly stopped bragging. And that's exactly why you shouldn't fish for spawning smallmouth. All those elements that make fly fishing so satisfying—the challenge of stealth, the art of the cast, the nuances of presentation—are lost on spawning fish, which are robotically required to dispatch of any and all intruders, no matter what. The only creature a spawning smallmouth can't defend its nest against is you.

If you simply must fish during the spawn, there are ways to do so ethically and responsibly—by recognizing smallmouth spawning habitat and/or avoiding presentation techniques that exploit spawning fish. Instead of fishing to shallow, off-channel flats and structure, concentrate your efforts on the second shelf, mid-channel seams, and places of quicker current where actively feeding pre-spawn fish will lie in ambush. As far as presentations go, fishing

The guides at Tight Lines Fly Fishing always pause their guide season for two weeks during the peak of the spawn, thus ensuring quality fishing on their best waters for years to come. NATE SIPPLE

unweighted baitfish imitations aggressively will ensure your fly is not bouncing through a nest. The same holds true for fishing small topwaters, since those nest marauders that smallmouth are programmed to defend against most often attack from below.

This brings us to post-spawn fish. These fish tend to inhabit what we refer to as "transitional water"—not quite as shallow and sequestered as the spawning beds, and not as fast as water preferred by pre-spawn and fully recuperated summer fish (post-spawn fish need a little protection once they leave the spawning bays and flats). The post-spawn period gets mixed reviews by many smallmouth anglers, and it will differ year to year according to weather patterns. When Bart and Tim were growing up in northern Wisconsin, the prevailing wisdom was that post-spawn fishing was the most difficult period of the year, with all the big females going off the feed to recover. That said, our observations over the decades suggest that this is not entirely true. While we do tend to note an absence of the larger females during this time, at any given moment toward the end of the spawn there's usually a mix of females going into recovery, as well as post-recovery females putting their feedbags on. One particularly memorable post-spawn day happened a number of years ago when Tim was guiding longtime clients and friends Bob Harrison and Michael Rock. They stumbled onto a pool that was five feet deep with a distinct shelf and caught numerous large fish in succession. It was easy to tell that these were post-spawn hens: They possessed a slightly milkier mucous membrane in addition to a flabby, eggless belly. Catching these fish was all about location. That slower, deeper, baitfish-filled water directly adjacent to a spawning flat was the perfect place for bass to recuperate after a rigorous spawning season.

SUMMER DIFFUSION

Summer is a big fat sweet spot for the smallmouth angler. It's at this time that fish will spread out through the river, aligning themselves with a variety of microhabitats. Their movements will no longer be seasonal migrations over acres or miles but rather daily movements in more closely circumscribed environments. And their goals in life will be very much simplified: eating, resting, eating again.

Because fish are so diffused during the summer, in this section we'll introduce a variety of vocabulary to describe quality smallmouth structure. But before we go into the full catalog of spots, we feel it's important to encourage smallmouth anglers to develop "spot vision." Spot vision is the faculty of recognizing the common features of smallmouth ambush habitat. One thing many of the following spots have in common is that they are points of contrast between two elements, and it's this contrast that affords a predator advantage over its prey. Contrasting elements may be current, temperature, depth, even

Summer is a time of high metabolism and great fishing opportunity. The warmer the temperatures, the more calories smallmouth bass need to eat on a daily basis. All this good eating results in healthy, acrobatic fish, such as this fine Wisconsin River specimen. ERIC CHRISTENSEN

light. Hiding behind a rock at the edge of faster current, a bass gets more cracks at food coming downriver without expending calories. A fish cloaked in shadow looking out into a well-lit portion of riverbed has the advantage of "prospect and refuge"—the ability to see without the possibility of being seen. Shelves, too, give actively feeding bass the opportunity of hunting shallower water while maintaining quick recourse to the safety of the deep. In the smallmouth's kitchen, these points of advantage are one half of the recipe for an easy meal. All that's needed is food, be it fly or flesh.

One other important point of emphasis before we proceed regards the best time to really learn your water: Hands-down the best time to learn a river in all its nuance and complexity is when it's low and clear, usually in late summer. So dedicate some of your late-summer time to surveying the scene and really getting to know your water. Even if you end up fishing less, you will be increasing your own predatory advantage by a significant margin.

Last but not least, one important thing to remember about smallmouth is their tendency to eat more the warmer the water gets. Despite being considered a "cool-water" fish, smallmouth only become more active during the hottest part of the summer. Dave remembers a blistering stretch of summer where temperatures climbed above ninety degrees for twelve days straight. At its peak, the surface temperatures of his local river registered eighty-five degrees. Every species of fish was on lockdown—except for smallmouth bass.

With their metabolisms tied to temperature, they turned into veritable eating machines during this heat wave, attacking baitfish and crayfish imitations with a frightening ferocity. We often tell our clients that the best weather for smallmouth is the most uncomfortable weather for us. If we have to jump in the river for a swim to cool down, it's going to be a good day of smallmouth fishing.

Now let's take a look at the structure and cover smallmouth relate to for a majority of the fishing season.

SHELVES

Shelves are tremendously important structure. When it comes to smallmouth bass rivers, we generally refer to two different shelves: the first and second. The first shelf is the water directly off the bank—those few feet of water extending from the bank until the first drop-off. Because minnows, crayfish, frogs, dragonflies, and damselflies congregate here, the first shelf is an important feeding area whenever there is enough water to make bass feel safe. The first shelf is also a go-to place during a high-water event, when holding flush to the bank is the only way for bass to escape heavy, whorling flows.

The transition between the first and second shelf can be a great place to target neutral, mid-afternoon fish. While drifting topwaters along the y-axis from a moving drift boat is one way to approach these fish, another is to fish from a wading position on the first shelf, casting toward the center of the river and swinging crayfish or sculpin patterns slowly back toward the transition zone. NATE SIPPLE

During such moments of high water be on the lookout for "flow transitions" on the first shelf. Typically found within a foot or two of the bank, this is where the flow goes from barely moving or still, to moving just a bit. It's amazing how often you'll find fish in this transitional spot.

The second shelf becomes a primary structure during low summer flows when the first shelf doesn't hold enough water for fish to feel safe. The second shelf provides three key factors: close proximity to food (typically found shallow), current relief from elements found on the shelf (rocks, wood, etc.), and cover via depth. This last part is important. Depth is in fact a form of cover for smallmouth bass. A fish with three feet of water above its head knows it has protection from an osprey or eagle. Water clarity plays a factor here as well. In general, fish in ultraclear water need more depth to feel secure than fish in murkier water.

Even during times when there is plenty of water on the first shelf, neutral fish will hang out on the edge of the second shelf between meals. This makes the drop to the second shelf a great place to target fish midday; though not actively feeding, they may well be open to investigating a potential meal. Laying anchor or taking up a casting position off to the side of the drop and quarter-casting to the bank side of the shelf with an attractive surface bug can peak interest from neutral fish. Oftentimes you will find a fish willing to creep up and look at your offering but sink back in refusal like a spring-creek trout. Backing up and revisiting the same neutral fish with a leech or crayfish can often seal the deal. Where the drop between the first and second shelf is sharper (a drop of two to four feet), try chugging a big diver to get a reaction. It can be amazing how at midday fish that aren't visibly feeding will many times tap into the carnal instincts that make them kill, seemingly for no other reason than because they can.

CURRENT SEAMS

Like most fish that make their living in rivers, smallmouth love being close to fast-moving water that brings food to them. But they don't want to be *too* close—the expenditure of energy is just too great out in the main flow. Thus, the position of greatest predatory advantage is the seam. From the soft side of the seam a bass can window-shop the fast, food-filled water just inches away. If something tasty and nutritious whooshes by, it's easily snatched up.

Current seams can be caused by just about anything: wood, rocks, sharper inside bends, bridge pilings, etc. Unfortunately, fishing seams effectively is not as easy as identifying them. The right casting position and deft line control are essential to successfully presenting to seams. The following illustration demonstrates that there are many wrong ways, and really only one right way, to approach a seam. Ideally, a fly should fall in the fish's field of vision and

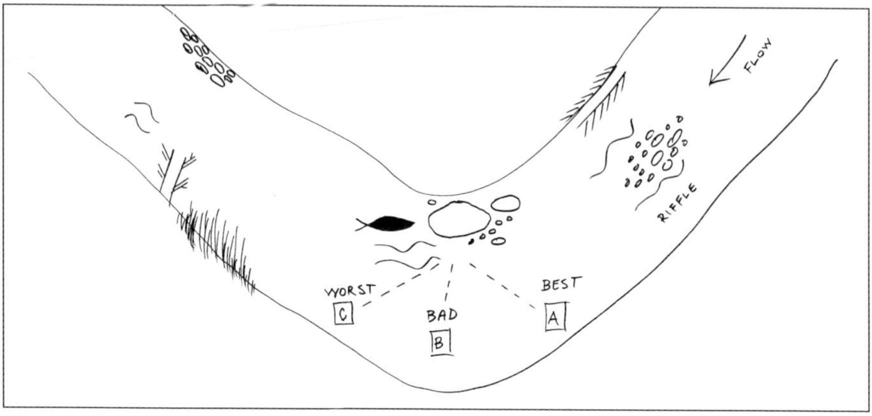

Whether presenting from a moving boat there's only one best place to present to a narrow seam window, and that's from upstream and at an angle (Position A). From here a reach cast will allow the fly to land upstream right in the fish's line of sight and hang enticingly in front of its face for a second or two. Position B is less far from ideal but can still work if water depth or overhanging branches prevent a presentation from Position A. Position C is by far the worst, and is usually the result of an angler trying to salvage a missed cast from Position A. While a fish may still chase, hook up ratios drop precipitously, as the down-and-away pull of the current makes it very hard for a fish to get the hook in its mouth. DAVE KARCZYNSKI

Current seams attract actively feeding fish, and thus should be worked thoroughly. Fish will hold on the slow side of the seam, waiting to ambush disoriented foodstuffs coming downstream in the quicker water. If a seam is long, prioritize those places where the seam intersects cover or structure. NATE SIPPLE

then hang there for a moment, giving the fish time to react to a fly before the fly darts away. Dropping bugs right on the soft side of the transition with a big aerial reach mend can buy enough time to get a reaction—and a hookup. Bass will often still give a slashing strike when a fly is being dragged away, but your odds of hooking up with that fish are greatly decreased. Since seams are some of the most consistent fish-holding spots during the summer months, it's well worth it to practice precision fly placement on your reach casts. Seams are where anglers with the best line-management skills will score.

RIFFLES

Riffles are stretches of relatively fast, shallow, broken water that occur as a result of gradient changes in a river. They play a major role in the river ecosystem. Whether on a trout stream or in a smallmouth river, broken riffle water allows oxygen from the air to permeate the river, creating a microhabitat rich with life; caddis flies, stone flies, mayflies, and midges all spend their early life in and around riffles. These microfauna attract small baitfish and crustaceans, which attract smallmouth bass—hence the importance of riffles to the smallmouth angler. The abundance of dissolved oxygen in and below riffles also means that fish will breathe easily even during the hottest times of the year. Finally, the fast water in and below riffles means that ambush lies in the form of current seams are abundant and easy to identify. In short, if your smallmouth river has riffles, you will want to spend plenty of time parsing and exploring them.

That said, smallmouth (or at least adult smallmouth) don't relate to riffles in the same way that trout do. Full-grown bass do not typically push into fast, shallow water to feast on nymphs. Instead, it's the hundred or so yards *below* riffles that are of primary importance to the smallmouth angler, particularly the point at which a shallow riffle empties into deeper water. Of course, there are exceptions to this rule as well. Bart was once taught a valuable lesson regarding the way larger bass sometimes use riffles. It was an early evening in late summer and he was pushing the boat hard through the shallow water in order to make up for lost time—to him, this particular riffle had always been fly-over country. Suddenly he saw a large bass crashing through the shallows just downstream, spraying baitfish out in front of him as though they'd been fired from a shotgun. Bart immediately dropped anchor and surveyed the scene as the fish cracked again. The riffle water in question was about fifty yards above a deeper holding lie, and it was easily apparent that the fish had slid upstream to have his supper. After slipping out of the boat to get into a better casting position, Bart swung a small crippled baitfish pattern through the area and was immediately fast to an especially angry eighteen-inch fish (there's something about the cramped quarters of the riffle that truly upsets smallmouth). Since that evening, this particular riffle and others like it have given up a number of fish in the upper-teener class.

Riffles are essential to the larger river ecosystem, providing oxygen that sustains the smallest and largest organisms in the system. While juvenile fish may be found in the quicker, shallow water, larger fish will usually be found toward the end of a riffle, where the water begins to slow down and gain depth. Swinging baitfish patterns in the quick water can induce ferocious takes, but take warning: An adult smallmouth moving downstream in quick water is a difficult creature to turn. Make sure your rod is stout and your tippet strong enough to play a serious fish in heavy flows. NATE SIPPLE

The moral of the story? While the few hundred yards below a riffle are always worth fishing, in those cases where riffles immediately dump into deep water, it's sometimes worth fishing the skinny stuff as well.

FEEDING FLATS

Feeding flats—large, relatively shallow areas of uniform depth—are typically features of larger rivers. If we had to conjure an image of the "ideal" feeding flat it would be between one and three feet deep with steady, even flows. It's this very predictability that makes flats an attractive hunting ground for bass. The evenness of the terrain means a hunting bass has visual access to a significant part of the flat at all times. And the uniformity of flow means that fish can cruise efficiently—that is, in a single gear—as they seek out food. But not all productive feeding flats fall into the "ideal flat" category. Sometimes a productive flat might be closer to four or five feet—or so shallow you wonder how bass can traverse it without beaching themselves. And while moderate current is ideal, slower flats can still be productive, and faster flats also offer good hunting provided there are boulders or other structure to break up the flows. The takeaway? More so than current speed and actual depth, it's the flatness of the flat that makes it a key feature. But, of course, there also has to be food present. Which brings us to our next point.

Different flats feature different foodstuffs and are thus more or less productive at different times of day and different times of year. Some rocky flats always have abundant crayfish and tend to be predictably productive when the bite is on—particularly in the evening, when crayfish become quite active and the softening light makes smallmouth feel more comfortable in shallow water. Other flats fish well only when a more seasonal prey item, like damselflies, is present in high numbers. Some flats with diverse menus will fish well all season, while others will be better at different times of year. Treat each flat like a different world, and try to get a sense of what food is present at what time of year.

Because flats tend to act as echo chambers of both sound and light, they are best approached in an understated fashion with smaller, softer flies. Drifting with an attractor pattern is a great way to approach flats fish. Set long reach mends with small surface flies in order to really let your fly "marinate" in the flat, with little more than a subtle pop or infrequent twitch. Don't overplay the fly: When fish are shallow and on the feed, their senses are on the highest alert. They know your fly is there. Less is much, much more.

Large expanses of uniform depth offer the bass a great hunting environment, in large part because the bass can use its vision and lateral line to perceive prey from a distance. This means it will also be able to more easily perceive you, the angler. Therefore, approach feeding flats stealthily with controlled casts that start closer to your wading position and gradually reach farther toward the back of the flat. If you catch a fish from the farthestmost part of the flat on your very first cast, it will probably be the only fish you take. ERIC CHRISTENSEN

While an evening of active flats fishing can redeem an otherwise humdrum day, flats shouldn't be saved for only evenings. On flats with significant wood or boulders, fish may be laid up all day long. Moving slowly and pushing very little wake will allow for some ultratechnical midday sight-fishing opportunities to fish using flats structure as a resting area. It's in presenting to these neutral, midday flats fish that casting and mending become especially paramount: These fish will not move nearly as far to take a fly as an actively feeding flats fish. However, if you can spot a good bass and make a precise drift right over its head, it will frequently tip its head back and accept a spontaneous snack.

We've also noticed other differences between hunting evening flats fish and those laid up midday: While actively feeding flats fish will typically respond to a variety of offerings, the flats fish of the afternoon tend to prefer more realistic imitations, particularly when water is low and clear. Damsels, small chernobyls, hoppers, and even crickets work great for these most *trutta*-like of smallmouth bass. It's true that midday flats fish can be difficult for beginning anglers, but make no mistake: Flats fish are hard-earned fish, and just one of them is worth ten fish caught blind-casting. The exponential satisfaction from a challenging flats fish is reason enough to keep your eyes sharp and peeled when moving through these shallow-water worlds in the afternoon.

Not only do tributary mouths concentrate fish, but sometimes the tributaries themselves can be worth exploring on foot. Wading upstream through the first few hundred yards of a good-size tributary can provide trout-style surface fishing with dead-drifted wigglies and poppers. NATE SIPPLE

TRIBUTARY MOUTHS

As mentioned earlier in this chapter, tributary mouths are especially important early and late in the season when creeks may be discharging warmer water into the system. Aside from temperature, however, tributary mouths offer other ambush opportunities such as seams where dirty water meets clear water, where two current edges come together, and where holes form at the river mouth. One great way to fish river mouths is to swing flies through these transition zones, especially early and late in the season.

WOOD

Wood comes in two varieties when it comes to smallmouth fishing. In high-gradient areas sweepers—or trees extending out into the main current perpendicular to shore—provide ambush opportunities in the same way that boulders and inside bends do. Active fish position themselves on the edges of these seams waiting for prey to be funneled their way. Sweepers in good flow tend to have two primary lies where actively feeding fish position themselves (denoted in the illustration below).

The other variety of wood comes in the form of submerged timber in slower-moving runs and flats. In these cases, timber serves as a resting area for smallmouth. Sunken timber in slow current can be especially important during times of low water. In shallow rivers where low-water bass might be without recourse to truly deep water, this type of wood attracts bass like a magnet. It can boggle the mind how several adult bass can hide in a relatively small outcropping of wood in a slow, sandy run. While fish hiding beneath

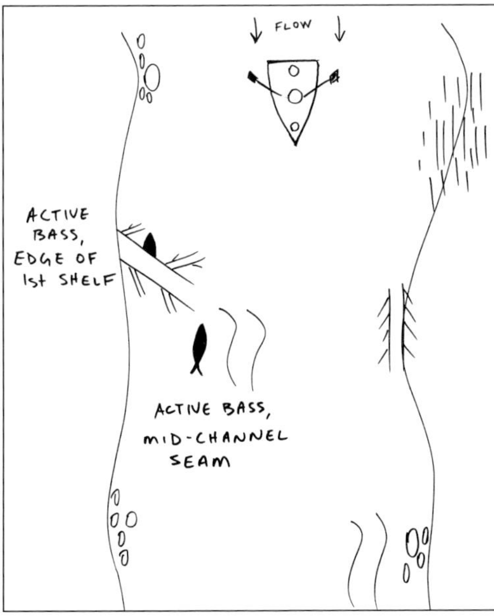

This illustration depicts the two main ambush points for bass when it comes to sweepers. While an angler fishing on foot can fish both lies, the boat angler often must choose one or the other. If there are two anglers in the boat, a strategy where the first angler fishes the mid-channel seam and the rear angler fishes the fish tucked away nearer the bank ensures that each sweeper gets fished to its maximum potential. DAVE KARCZYNSKI

wood in runs and on flats are not necessarily actively feeding fish, that doesn't mean they aren't open to a dinner invitation. Bumping and grazing such wood with slow-moving, shallow-running streamers (both smaller divers and lightly weighted streamers) is sometimes all that's needed to rouse multiple fish at the same time out of the same sunken log.

It can be shocking how many large bass can hide in what would seem to be tiny dark spaces among sunken timber. Sometimes the key to coaxing wary, low-water fish out of hiding is a soft-landing, slow-falling fly that grazes the wood as it's fished. NATE SIPPLE

Logjams offer refuge from current and good ambush points for prey items drifting past. Swinging a mid-column pattern across the face of the logjam, from the shallow side to the deep, ensures that every ambushing bass in the vicinity will see your fly. Odds are at least one will be a player. NATE SIPPLE

RIPRAP, WOOD SEAWALLS, AND SHEER ROCK FACES

We're lumping these three structural features together because all are vertically oriented and smallmouth tend to relate to them in the same way.

First, let's talk riprap. If you've got houses along your beat of river, odds are that you've got riprap. Riprap attracts and holds crayfish—and in turn smallmouth. Especially on more developed, suburban rivers that may suffer from silty bottoms, riprap can be a smallmouth magnet. On some larger rivers, riprap may extend for dozens or hundreds of yards, but even a short strip of riprap several feet long is well worth your best presentation. No matter how big it is, a strip of riprap will hold fish.

Sometimes the fish-drawing power of riprap can transcend location as well. One instance illustrates this to an extreme degree. Dave was fishing a fairly large oxbow lake well off the main river channel. It was classic largemouth bass and pike territory, and neither Dave nor his fishing partner had smallmouth on the mind that day. Then they noticed that amid all the hundreds of yards of milfoil, mulch, and lily pads, a homeowner had dredged a slot for his boathouse and protected his shoreline with riprap. On the very first cast, the riprap yielded a gigantic smallmouth that, until it breached, both anglers took for a bowfin or carp. Now the spot was at least a thousand yards from any

Provided there's sufficient depth, riprap concentrates crayfish—and therefore smallmouth bass—and is thus always worthy of your sustained presentation efforts. NATE SIPPLE

current flow whatsoever, but food was present in the form of crayfish. This small patch of riprap is now good for exactly one smallmouth per outing.

Sheer rock faces and wood seawalls are a little different in terms of how fish use them. Whereas riprap fish are generally looking to pop crayfish, sheer rock

Whether it's composed of natural or man-made materials, a sheer vertical structure allows bass to hunt baitfish efficiently. Bass will chase schools of minnows into the wall, then snatch their disoriented bodies when the prey runs out of room for escape. If you see fresh splash marks against the side of a sheer wall, you know bass are on the feed. NATE SIPPLE/DAVE KARCZYNSKI

faces and wood seawalls help bass hunt baitfish. Bass will herd baitfish into the vertical structure and then take advantage of their disorientation when they run out of room to escape. If you see minnows going airborne along a wood seawall or rock face, odds are there's a predator on the hunt just below.

What all three of these structures have in common is their verticality, which means target fishing zones may be small. Fish will often hang suspended just a few feet off the structure. One effective way to approach vertical structure is with topwaters and a dropper. Another way is to fish the fall—that is, to throw lightly weighted patterns right up onto the structure and then slowly walk them down the drop toward waiting fish. You might not have to wait long. When fishing riprap and sheer rock faces, be prepared for near-instantaneous strikes. Flies with reversed hooks (hook point riding up instead of down) definitely aid in walking flies down rock steps without hanging up.

WHAT TO AVOID: FROG WATER

Up to now we've been preoccupied with what water *to* fish. Now we're going to talk about the water *not* to fish. Yes, it's time to discuss that most questionable type of smallmouth water—"frog water." Experienced anglers know it when they see it. Suddenly the river slows, and there is nothing that looks fishy—no current seams, no holes, no shelves toward which the caster can direct his efforts. The bottom becomes dark with silt and marl. If there are rocks on the bottom, they are covered with several inches of silt. If you're wading, you will experience frog water not just visually but viscerally: You'll sink into sucking muck and may or may not emerge with your boot. With thick, scummy weeds and a not-so-fresh odor in the air, you may feel like you are suddenly on a different river. You catch a fish that feels heavy but nonetheless fights like a wet rag—it's a largemouth. Your popper disappears below the surface—then disappears from your line. You've been bitten off by a pike.

There are a number of reasons why frog water fails to hold significant populations of smallmouth, but the most significant is an absence of smaller foodstuffs that feed larger foodstuffs. Whatever cobble may have once existed has been buried by silt, so forget about crayfish. And the slow flows result in relatively low levels of dissolved oxygen—not great habitat for most nymphs, and not great habitat for smallmouth themselves during the summer when water temperatures are high.

And so frog water is always pass-over water. Okay: almost always.

One particular instance got us thinking about *certain* frog water differently. A few years ago, Charlie had a young angler in the boat. He was a very mature thirteen-year-old and could flat out fish like a machine. He and Charlie were working their way into the mouth of a side channel on a perfect June day. The left side of the channel was the obvious good water; it had the right amount

This early season fish came from an expanse of slack water with a mucky bottom. Usually this would be pass-over water, but amphibians were in their spring migration mode up and down the river corridor, and this fish found itself in the midst of a mother lode of spring peepers. NATE SIPPLE

of flow, depth, and structure. The right side, by contrast, had a grassy point, black mud bottom, no flow to speak of, and a thick patch of lily pads—the very definition of "frog water." Against Charlie's recommendation, the young angler fired his popper right up to that patch of lily pads. The water promptly exploded, and Charlie waited for his six-dollar fly to be sawed off by the inevitable pike. Lo and behold, it was not an *Esox* but a large smallmouth. After releasing the fish Charlie went out to inspect the area and concluded it had been the scene of intense damselfly nymph activity—it was the right time of year for it.

Our takeaway was this: Just as riffle water can be productive provided it's adjacent to deeper water, so can frog water that abuts cooler, cleaner, faster smallmouth habitat hold fish—but only if one of their preferred foods is available in high volume.

FALL PODDING

Something happens as summer nears its end. Surface water temps that have lingered near eighty degrees for months begin to drop. As August turns to September, days become shorter and nights become cooler. As warm-blooded animals, we humans swap shorts and sandals for long pants and boots. When the trees are just starting to show the first signs of change, the fish start to change their behavior, too. People go to their favorite piece of smallmouth water and begin to catch fewer and fewer bass. The popular assumption is that the fish are done feeding for the year. We've even heard old-timers say that when smallmouth feel the water start to cool, they just sink right to the bottom and sit there, like a big, lazy flathead catfish. But in actuality these fish are far from done feeding; they're just doing it in a different location.

Studies have shown that in most river systems, smallmouth begin to move within a week to ten days of the autumnal equinox. Throughout much of the bass's range, this corresponds with water temperatures falling into the sixties. That's when popular summer haunts of the smallmouth bass are abandoned in favor of other waters. With everything in the bass's world changing all around them, bass no longer have incentive to remain in their summer haunts. Surviving the imminent fall and winter means seeking out microhabitats where conditions are more hospitable to a bass's winter metabolism. This typically means an area where water conditions are as stable as possible. Flows, water temps, and food must be as consistent and predictable. More often than not, this easy living means an area in a river system with greater than average depth, though by no means does this always mean downstream. In fact, smallmouth in impounded systems often migrate upstream to deep pools below dams.

Instead of roaming shallow flats, fall smallmouth will favor deeper shorelines with slow current, wide pools, and deep eddies. By the time water temperatures get into the fifties, most fish have established themselves in the area where they'll spend the next five to seven months. How far they'll migrate depends on several factors, such as the size of the river and the concentration of fish. In deeper river systems with low concentrations of smallmouth, this might mean traveling only a very short distance. In shallow rivers with greater concentrations of fish, this could mean traveling upwards of ten miles or more. On a study of Wisconsin's Wolf and Embarrass Rivers, smallmouth were observed to swim a shocking seventy miles to find suitable wintering water. This means that in order to be successful this time of the year, anglers have to be flexible and ready to move, much like our quarry.

On some river systems, you'll be able to take fish on the surface well into the fall, while on others you'll have to go strictly subsurface as soon as the first cool nights hit. Whether or not your river fishes well on the surface in early autumn generally relates to the local frog populations. On river systems that experience a substantial autumn frog migration, autumn anglers can catch their largest fish of the season up top, while those on other rivers might have a difficult time finding fish to hook and might have to resort to pursuing podding fish farther down in the water column. The only way to find out how the fish in your system behave in the fall is to fish them.

Fall means different things on different river systems. Fish on heavily impounded rivers may travel only a few hundred yards toward wintering habitat, while fish on free-flowing systems may travel up to one hundred miles or more. Depending on the patterns of fish in your system, you may find yourself focusing more on transitional water or deeper holes as water temperatures drop and fall sets in. NATE SIPPLE

Eventually even sustained topwater bites come to an end, at which point anglers will have to finish the smallmouth season by going subsurface. After the topwater bite ends we like an intermediate line with slow-moving, neutrally buoyant baitfish patterns. When fished on intermediate lines, flies such as the Murdich Minnow and Barto Minnow, which we fish fairly quickly in the summer, can be twitched slowly and then stopped in the water column, hanging in front of fish without dropping to the bottom. We've often seen large smallmouth in September follow a minnow pattern more than twenty feet, only to lazily inhale it on the pause. Once October rolls around, intermediate lines may have to be swapped for lines with an even faster sink rate. These lines, paired with a weighted fly such as a Clouser Minnow or a Whitlock's Deep Sheep Minnow, can bring positive results with the deep stripping techniques discussed later in this book. Dredging is also an option during this time of year. Where the water is less than ten feet deep, a long untapered leader with a crayfish pattern or large nymph fished under a strike indicator can also work very well. The bottom line is, slow your presentation down and work diligently through slower pools and deeper water. Carry multiple lines and flies with various sink rates to tip the odds in your favor. Be patient. The fish are there. They may just need a little more coaxing in the cooler months.

Understanding and Using Modern Data

Compared to lakes, rivers are dynamic environments. Floods and severe high-water events may change the fundamental composition and contour of a river, relocating sandbars, displacing trees, collapsing undercuts, and sometimes even moving boulders. There are smaller-scale changes as well, such as those changes in clarity and temperature following a good rain. And on certain impounded rivers, dam releases may occur multiple times within a day, meaning hourly fluctuations will be something you want to be privvy to. The important thing to remember is that the river you fished on Saturday might not be the river you fish on Sunday.

To help get a clearer sense of your river's different personalities, we encourage you to make notes of the gauge height and flow rate (measured in cubic feet per second, or cfs) every time you go out, especially if this practice is new to you. Gauge height will give you an idea of where you might be able to go on foot and in a boat. Very low water means your watercraft might have trouble passing through the shallow stretches (you might have

Rain events and dam releases can change the character of a river quite suddenly. By studying USGS flow patterns on a regular basis, you can gain a better idea of how your river system responds to precipitation—without even having to be on the water. NATE SIPPLE

to get out and drag the boat), while very high water might mean that wading anglers need to be extra cautious and hew to the bank when passing deeper holes. In most states, navigability laws enable wading anglers to bypass dangerously deep or fast water by a quick foray onto private land; to keep this privilege intact, respect landowner rights and keep use of private land to a minimum.

Likewise, understanding flow rates will help you make informed decisions about whether to wade upstream or down (or fish at all), and will help you anticipate where you can expect to find fish—the harder the flows, the tighter to structure fish will be. For the boat angler, cfs will help you estimate how fast or slow you can expect your float time to be. The time it takes to float and fish six miles of river can vary quite a bit depending on how much water is in the system.

Be mindful when checking river data. Your river may very well have several USGS gauges on it. If this is the case, be sure to refer to the gauge closest to the water you are fishing, since rivers are also dynamic through the length of their flows, depending on the gradient of the surrounding environment. And while rivers typically slow down as they move toward their ends, this is not a uniform change. There will be slow stretches of river and fast stretches of river scattered all throughout a river system.

It's important to remember that while river data can be useful, it also doesn't have to be your destiny. A number of years ago the shop had the opportunity to shoot a video with famed fly-fishing videographer and friend R. A. Beattie. R. A. was working on his video *Off the Grid* and was hoping to capture something for the upcoming fly-fishing film tour for his entry. As the hosting shop and outfitter, Tight Lines was very excited at the opportunity to get their fishery on film. But excitement turned to terror as Tim stood in the garage of the guide house watching the rain hammer the drift boats in the yard. This was the worst-case scenario for having a camera crew aboard for a day of fishing. All of the guides watched intently at the USGS gauge as it shot from its normal summer flows of 1,500 cfs to 8,000 cfs overnight.

Fortunately, the watershed in question flows through very little agriculture land, and so remains reasonably clear during high water. Many rivers that run through farmland would simply turn to mud and be mostly unfishable. That being said, it was still very scary pushing the boats off the ramp for the shoot. Lucky for the crew, even with the huge bump in water the fishing was absolutely lights-out! With the massive push of water following the storm forced all the bass in the system out of the main flow, making bank fishing spectacular.

On the flip side of this scenario, on impounded rivers you can see the water fall nearly as quickly as it had risen. When water levels that have been stable at 5,000 cfs suddenly fall to 1,200 cfs, you may have a problem. The shallow-water haunts for the smallmouth disappear again, and fish find sanctuary in

The payoff for knowing how fish in your watershed respond to different water levels and flow rates? Quality fish in adverse conditions. Here, Tim shows off a popper-eating bass plucked from a blown-out river. The secret was landing large poppers hard within an inch of the bank—the only place bass could get relief from the heavy current. NATE SIPPLE

deeper water. It does not take a long time for them to acclimate, but it can most certainly throw a bit of a monkey wrench into the first half of the day.

For all these reasons, USGS river gauges are among the most powerful tools modern anglers have at their disposal. These are readings taken at thousands of rivers around the country that identify a river's height relative to historical norms, as well as flow rates, measured in cubic feet per second, or cfs. Guides and savvy anglers are always checking the gauges in order to better anticipate the conditions they'll meet upon arriving at the river.

Checking gauges is important because a foot is not always a foot. How comfortable a smallmouth feels at a given depth has much to do with where water levels are relative to where water levels have been. If water has been low for weeks but is suddenly on the rise after an upstream rain event, fish are more likely to feel more comfortable in that single foot of water, making the first shelf and shallow feeding flats an attractive place to hunt. If, conversely, water levels have been dropping steadily for a long time, that foot of water may be viewed as a place of further constriction and danger. Knowing what your river has been up to relative to the immediate past as well as historical norms will help you think about where you're best off focusing your attention at the start of the day.

Rivers with regular dam discharges have a more irregular cfs line with sharp spikes and valleys. The outflux of water might result in sudden and dramatic changes in cfs. Some fisheries revolve entirely around the outflux of water—for examples Arkansas's White River, a trophy brown trout fishery. If you're on such a river, pay attention to flows throughout the day; it might make the difference between a good and mediocre day on the water.

On rivers controlled by dams, water releases that raise water levels just a bit tend to get baitfish and crayfish moving to find better cover and resting habitat—and this activates the smallmouth. Conversely, damn shutoffs that result in suddenly falling water tend to make fish nervous—and for good reason. Imagine for a moment that the house you lived in, without warning, began to shrink. What would you do? Probably abandon your everyday habits—like snacking all day long—and instead devote time to seeking out an area that's more stable and comfortable. At times of precipitously falling water levels, smallmouth do the exact same thing.

Rising flows can be just fine, especially if they rise slowly. This can open up a bunch of new holding and feeding water. It's a great time to fish creek mouths if the volume coming out of them is significant. Creek mouths with elevated flows in the summer are almost always a home run, as there tends to be a lot of food getting flushed into the main river.

Rivers are dynamic things and they require dynamic approaches. What worked one day might not work the next. Close observation and open-mindedness are necessary to be successful day in and day out on the water. NATE SIPPLE

Remember that rivers are complex watersheds that may drain a much larger area than you yourself may be familiar with. Just because it didn't rain on your beat of river doesn't mean thunderstorms on tributaries aren't going to affect your fishing. In fact, quite the opposite is true. The most significant water events are those that occur at the upper end of a watershed. An isolated rainstorm downstream will have no effect on the middle stretches. An isolated shower on the middle stretches will have a slight effect on the middle stretches and a bit more downriver. But rain at the headwaters of a system affects all of the river. Keep this in mind when watching the radar in preparation for a fishing trip.

Google Earth can also be a useful tool, especially for scouting new water. Unlike USGS data, which changes by the hour to reflect the most recent conditions, Google Earth images may be several months or years old. Even in the winter, Google Earth images show summer landscapes. This is not bad for the angler since midsummer tends to have stable flows. A trained eye can generally discern the time of year the image was taken. On certain rivers in northern Minnesota and Wisconsin, waterfalls are common, and Google Earth typically helps identify pitfalls for adventurous anglers looking to explore new and remote water.

Google Earth is also good for telling you what the surrounding environment consists of. Is there significant development where we might expect to encounter a good deal of man-made structure? If there isn't development on the river corridor itself, what does the surrounding area look like? Is it largely agrarian? In that case we might expect runoff.

Google Earth will also help you identify tributaries as well as their surrounding environments. All other things being equal, a tributary passing through open farmland is likely to be darker and warmer than a tributary passing through dense forest (where the understory will minimize runoff, and the tree cover will minimize solar heat). That said, there are other factors that determine temperature as well, so make it a point to take the temperatures of your tributaries at the first bridge crossing or public access upstream from the confluence. Do so in spring, summer, and fall so as to gain a full understanding of temperature patterns in relation to the main branch.

How to Approach High Water

This past summer Dave was learning some new water, a little-fished tributary on one our trademark smallmouth streams. The water was relatively low, and Day 1 saw great action on baitfish patterns fished down through the second shelf. That night saw a rain event thirty miles upriver, and though no rain fell near Dave's beat, the next day the river was higher and faster. Stubbornly determined to duplicate the success of the previous day, Dave spent the first half of the day throwing the same flies in the same way he had the day prior—to no avail. It wasn't until he accepted that this would be a much different day that he changed his approach, concentrating on hanging a popper and mini-Tequeely dropper in small, slack water pockets right along the bank. By the end of the float, he'd taken a handful of decent fish, redeeming the earlier part of the day. The lesson he learned? Fish the river that is, not the river that was.

Though it's more common early in the season, high water doesn't happen only in spring. Rain events and dam releases can create high water throughout the year. But how a given river responds to added water owes largely to the geological makeup of the surrounding areas. Rivers that flow through agricultural areas might expect more serious discoloration due to topsoil runoff. And rivers in paved urban and suburban areas may experience greater than average bumps in water height, since there is little vegetation to slow the flow of water. In highly developed areas, stormwater drainage systems may also play a factor. That all said, some of the better fishing we experience occurs after a good warm rain.

Bass in high, off-colored water might require extra help in locating a fly. Tying rattles into your patterns can boost your success rate when fish have to hunt more by sound than by sight. NATE SIPPLE

High water is big-fly time. Whether fishing surface or subsurface patterns, look for flies with oversize heads that push a lot of water. The greater the displacement of water, the easier time a bass will have dialing in on your offering. NATE SIPPLE

In the case of mild to moderate rain events, anglers should concentrate efforts where the recently added water enters directly into the river system: creek mouths, feeder streams, even culverts pumping water into the system. These types of places are likely to abound with disoriented baitfish. They are also likely to possess water clarity seams, where predatory fish lie in ambush in murkier water and hunt the slightly clearer water just a few feet away. In addition to confused baitfish, fish set up below water entry points will also feed on the worms, salamanders, mice, and other food that gets washed into the river. After a good rain we've seen creek-mouth smallmouth so full of worms they were squirming out their gill openings—and the smallmouth were still feeding. Where food and fish concentrate is where you should also concentrate your efforts. Anchor up on these spots and work them thoroughly.

In the case of a more serious rain event, finding the right current speed is more important than anything else. We catch a lot of fish in people's yards when high water overflows the banks, and that isn't because "fresh-mowed lawn" is preferred smallmouth structure. Rather, it just so happened that backyards were the only place where bass could find the current speed they were looking for. During the warmer months, high water can make for great popper fishing right up against the bank, since this may be the only place in the system where a fish can find relief from torrential currents. It can be like western hopper fishing, floating at high speed and smacking poppers on the small (sometimes less than one foot) cushion of water along the river's edge. Water that was previously not deep enough to pass oxygen through gills is now deep and soft enough to provide protection and easy living.

How to Approach Low Water

"How's the fishing?"

"We need a bump."

We need a bump. What does that mean, exactly?

During low water, the feeding flats and shallow shelves that once comfortably accommodated smallmouth now barely have enough water to cover a fish's back. Low water levels can affect a lot of things in a river, but first and foremost they affect a fish's general level of wariness. Skinny water brings all the dangers of the outside world that much closer to the fish—and there's plenty of danger. Over the course of its lifetime, an adult smallmouth is likely to have survived a close call—or two—from a heron, an otter, or an eagle. The fear of "death from above" is real, and never more so than during the skinny-water season.

Many anglers make the mistake of continuing to pound the bank when the water is low. They're happy to go about aimlessly throwing their poppers into two inches of water when all the fish are hanging off the drop by the boat. Bass will still relate to shallow water when water is low, but they will often sit on the drop-off instead of up on the flat or shelf.

This doesn't mean that bass don't use ultrashallow flats when it's time to feed. They do, especially in the evening, because more often than not this is where food concentrates. What it means is that they get pretty sensitive to any sort of anomaly—a boat displacing water, a wading angler pushing wake, a bird flying overhead. We have witnessed remarkable demonstrations of environmental awareness from skinny-water smallmouth bass. One particularly memorable moment came during a low-water period when Charlie was carefully working the outer edge of a shallow flat. The near bank had a few towering pine trees on it, and at the top of one of those trees loomed a single solitary bald eagle. While the bird sat in the tree, everything was fine. Fish went about their business stalking minnows and slurping crayfish. But the moment the eagle took to flight the flat literally exploded, with dozens of bass swimming away in every direction. That bird was easily one hundred feet above the water when it took off, but that was enough to spook the fish.

This was a perfect illustration of the importance of stealth in low water. Watch your casting, your boatwork, your wading, and your shadow.

While the above anecdote speaks to the challenges of low-water fishing, there are definite advantages to be had as well. First off, low water concentrates fish. If you know your river, you should know where to find water that's deep enough to harbor fish in ultralow-water periods even before you get to the river. Second, during low water a river can "speak" to an angler in ways it cannot when the banks are running full. By sitting on a high bank or climbing up on the rowers' seat, the patient angler can see deep into the smallmouth's world in ways that simply are not possible during higher water conditions. Low, clear water yields a direct view of fish, whether they're skulking behind boulders or drifting along a shelf. But low water doesn't have to be clear to betray fish position and behavior. In stained water, low-water fish still give themselves away in the form of nervous water or a swirl.

When you approach an area where you have evidence of smallmouth activity, start short and work your way out. We have clients who are great casters, and there's nothing they like more than to bomb a fly out to the back of a flat. It's often a fish that makes them do this: They are trying for that obvious waker

Low water may make moving through the river corridor and presenting flies more difficult (since fish can more easily detect the angler's presence), but it makes fish location a good deal easier, too. With conditions like this, fish will be crammed into whatever dark, deep water still remains. Fish these lies subtly and stealthily and you will be rewarded with good fishing. NATE SIPPLE

Damselflies and dragonflies can be great for prospecting in low, clear water when fish demand a more realistic imitation. How realistic an offering needs to be will vary by watershed. NATE SIPPLE

tucked way, way back. But even as they cast to that one distant fish, we'll see seven wakes blowing off the water and heading for the depths. Ninety-five percent of those fish are not going to come back. And the 5 percent that do return are no longer in feeding mode—they are in "staying alive" mode. So rather than casting to random fish, treat flats bass like you'd treat a pod of trout: Catch those fish close to you first and gradually work your way forward. Casting to skinny-water fish is a bit like working a genie—you only get so many wishes, and you can't wish for more. The key is to be patient, and whatever you do, *don't try to force feed a fish.* If a fish shows a negative reaction to a fly, stop presenting immediately. Give that fish time to settle down and try another fly: You'll do much more harm than good if you try to make it eat. You may not catch every fish on the flat, but if you play your cards right you'll catch more than just one.

Low water also ushers in the sight-fishing game, where the fishing is measured much more in quality than quantity. Low-water sight fishing is truly where smallmouth show how hard they can be to catch. Watching a fish react to your presentation, be it a fin-shimmy, a slight tip-up, or a backpedaling, nose-to-the-bug refusal, can be just as intense and exhilirating as an eat. We have spent hours in low water working a pod of laid-up fish, employing a lot more finesse than most people would ever consider necessary for smallmouth. Why would we choose to go through this dance of refusals and breath-holding exercise? Because it works. Just because the fish refuses one bug doesn't mean he's done. It only means that it's time to rerig, adjust your tippet, change your fly, refine your presentation. The only part better than seeing the fish slowly rise up and break the surface is the fury he kicks out with when he tastes that steel.

A Note on Bite Windows

If you fish a lot, you've noticed a phenomenon generally referred to as "bite windows," a period of time during which the fish, for some reason or other, suddenly go on the feed. You and your partner are fishing with nothing happening and then all of a sudden, you land a fish. Your partner misses one and then hooks up on the very next cast. A switch seems to have been flicked on. Maybe it's a microscopic change in flows, a bump in water temps, a fluctuation of barometric pressure, or Venus lining up perfectly with Saturn. Whatever the case, when a bite window is on, it's a time to make sure that your fly is in the water. It's not the time to be tinkering with leaders and flies, wrestling hooks out of trees, or eating a sandwich. Fish hard, make your casts count, and hold on.

Smallmouth guides sometimes live and die by these bite windows. When fish have collective lockjaw—and it does happen—it can make for a tough time on the water. But the good news is that there typically will be a good bite window at some point during the day. We've seen it thousands of times.

Sometimes it's only by covering a lot of water and fishing large, dynamic flies aggressively that neutral bass can be coaxed to eat. KYLE ZEMPEL

You've tried a bunch of different things during the first half of a float to little or know avail. Going into lunch with four fish in the net isn't a great deal of fun for either guides or anglers. Then, for reasons largely unknown, the fish begin to feed in the second half of the day.

When the bite is on, it can be otherworldly. The things smallmouth will do for a meal lend greatly to their status as a game fish. It's not uncommon to have multiple takes on a surface fly as it's dragging along between casts, or for one fish to pluck a fly out of another's mouth. At times like this it feels like you can do no wrong. A perfect example of this happened one day a few years back when Charlie was out with a longtime Oregon steelhead guide and his son. They were having a decent day, but then all of a sudden the fish just exploded. Several fish were landed in succession. Both anglers caught fish on consecutive casts. At one point the son was preparing to cast and had flipped his line over the side of the boat. His fly line and leader were a mess of spaghetti with the fly and tippet right at the center. Suddenly, a bass materialized from below and rose up right underneath the fly and ate it up in the midst of that stringy mess. It was one of the neatest tricks we've ever seen a smallmouth do.

That all said, smallmouth fishing isn't always peaches and cream. Bite doors can be as real as bite windows, and it's at these times that an angler has to work harder than usual to coax a smallmouth to eat. Kelly Galloup has compared aggressive streamer tactics for predatory fish to a grizzly bear encounter. If you have the misfortune of startling a grizzly bear, the last thing you should ever do is run; running can trigger the predator/prey response, and a bear that had no real interest in eating you may well attack because his DNA has taken over the wheel. The same is true for smallmouth bass. Try slamming a large streamer in their face and making it flee quickly—this oftentimes turns an otherwise sleepy fish into a killer.

CHAPTER 3

The Surface

Game fish come equipped with a variety of different jaw structures, each of which tells a different story about how these fish evolved to hunt prey. Some species, like the channel catfish, have an obvious overbite—useful in pinning prey and other things on the bottom. The brook trout has a jaw that occupies much of its face—the hinge extends back even beyond the eye—a testament to how it evolved to eat during the relatively short growing season of northern latitudes and high country streams. Then there's the smallmouth bass. A look at its jaw structure shows a lower jaw that extends beyond the upper. The biology tells the story of a fish that evolved to feed up top.

Very few folks need to be convinced to tie on a topwater fly for smallmouth. That's because topwater fishing has got something for everyone. Great casters can be virtuosic with long-distance aerial mends. Beginning casters can work on lengthening their drifts with on-the-water mending. And, on a good day, everyone has a chance at a good eat, no matter their skill set. We have some clients

When the surface game is on, there are few better places to be than on your favorite smallmouth river with a box of topwater flies and a few good friends. MICHAEL LESCHISIN

so devoted to the topwater that it's hard to get them to fish anything else—even when they definitely should be. Nate remembers one particularly difficult day on the water early in the season. He had started his clients on topwaters and then gone to the middle column, both to no avail. As Nate was about to tie on a dredging rig, the client interjected and pointed at a Boogle Bug. "If I'm not going to catch fish," he said, "I'd like to not catch fish with a popper on."

One of the great draws to smallmouth bass fishing is the topwater eat. Whether characterized as a toilet bowl *swoosh* or a subtle, deliberate sip, the surface eat is one of the things that makes the smallmouth bass so exciting and rewarding as fly rod quarry—but it's not that visual drama alone that motivates us to fish on the surface. In addition to the drama of the eat, topwater flies also give you perhaps your best chance at the fish of a lifetime—that's right, not baitfish patterns or crayfish but topwaters. Indeed, our observations over the decades lead us to believe that fishing up top is about catching the biggest of big smallmouth.

We have a theory that certain much-larger-than-average smallmouth are not full-time crayfish eaters. That's because crayfish are not exactly the most efficient food source when it comes to digestion, though they are the most

A proper popper box will have a variety of different bugs for different conditions. When assembling your popper box, look for flies of different sizes, profiles, head shapes, and color. This will ensure that you have the right sound for the occasion, be it a baritone bloop to call fish up from deeper structure or a subtler pop for whispering to fish in shallow, clear water. NATE SIPPLE

available. The fact is there's a lot of wasted energy produced while digesting these large crustaceans (think of how hard a bass's body has to work to process and expel all those exoskeletons and carapaces). Higher up in the water column, however, bass can find many things that are denser in quality nutrients. Damselflies: more nutrients. Mice and voles: more nutrients. Frogs: a whole lot more nutrients. The quality of the protein found in preystuffs that live at the surface is one way to explain the observation that all—not "some" or "most" but *all*—of the twenty-two-inch fish we've caught over the course of our careers have come on topwaters. As such we feel confident stating that truly large fish feed efficiently on the most nutritious flesh, which comes from above.

The surface might look to the angler like an easy nut to crack, but in fact the opposite is true. Perhaps nowhere else in the water column does the how, why, and when of smallmouth fishing have so many different nuances and possibilities.

The When

First, let's talk about the when. In northern Wisconsin where we do most of our guiding and fishing, we have a tradition of obsessing over the first topwater fish of the year. How do we know when it's time to start trying for that first telltale fish? While river temperatures provide a rough guide, and fifty degrees marks the conventional start point (spring) and end point (fall) for successful topwater fishing, we often rely on the mood of the fish to dictate our approach. This means paying attention to cues that arrive to us during the course of a day's fishing.

Here's a look at the progression of cues we'll pay attention to in deciding when to start throwing topwater flies in the spring. We usually start the season via vertical dredging and deep swinging. After several days (or weeks, depending on the weather) of early season smallmouth fishing with weighted flies, we start to notice that flies are getting intercepted midway on their initial fall to the bottom—a cue that fish are getting more aggressive. It's at that time that we make our first major change in where we're targeting fish in the water column. We can now start swimming baitfish imitations higher up in the column, from just off the bottom to the middle column. This may go on for a week or two, depending on conditions. Then, one day, things start to change.

The cues start subtly. One day, around midday when the water is starting to warm, we'll get a particularly long follow on a baitfish pattern. When a fish moves a considerable distance to take a look at the fly, this tells us that something has changed in the mood and the metabolism of a fish. They are

How long it takes a fish to react to a topwater fly in its vicinity will depend on a number of factors, with water temperature being foremost. The colder the water, the longer you should work a topwater fly before giving up on a cast. Even curious fish may need some time to move a few yards when metabolism is slow. That said, when the water heats up, be prepared for near-instant strikes. KYLE ZEMPEL

getting curious. It doesn't even matter if a fish doesn't end up eating the fly; all we want to see is that the fish will move a distance to have a look at our offering. When this threshold of curiosity is crossed, we know we can generally get a fish to eat a popper.

Then there are the not-so-subtle cues that topwater time is upon, say, a baitfish imitation getting eaten the minute it splashes down on the water, before the first strip is made. Once this happens, you not only can throw topwater flies, you should have started throwing them a week or two ago. Year in and year out, topwater fish come much earlier than people think. But they won't come from the quick water, or the deeper water. Rather, the first topwater eat of the year will generally come from the slow, greasy water that is slightly warmer than all the water around it.

As a side note, we'll mention that in this chapter we'll be concerning ourselves with "true" topwater flies, which is to say poppers, wigglies, sliders, and insect imitations. Even though they land on the surface and come to rest there between strips, we'll use divers as our segue to discussing the middle part of the water column. They will make up the first part of "The Middle Column" chapter.

Types of Topwater Flies

In order to group topwater flies in different categories, we first have to take into account the nuances of fishing the surface. First off, the surface is a mysterious place. It's a kind of portal, and a mystery to the creatures on either side of it, whether they be mammals or fish. For us human anglers, it's a barrier to another world where our quarry lives—we want to get to the other side, which we view as a place of excitement, possibility, and fun. For the bass, it's a barrier to another world where high-quality food is available, but there's a catch—it's also where their primary predators live. It's a place of danger, danger, and more danger. Imagine a restaurant where the food was easy to get but where each excursion brought with it the threat of annihilation. You can see why smallmouth bass are by nature wary of what's on the other side. Simply put, the surface is where a fish negotiates its willingness to eat with its wariness of death from above. These complex tensions emerging at the nexus

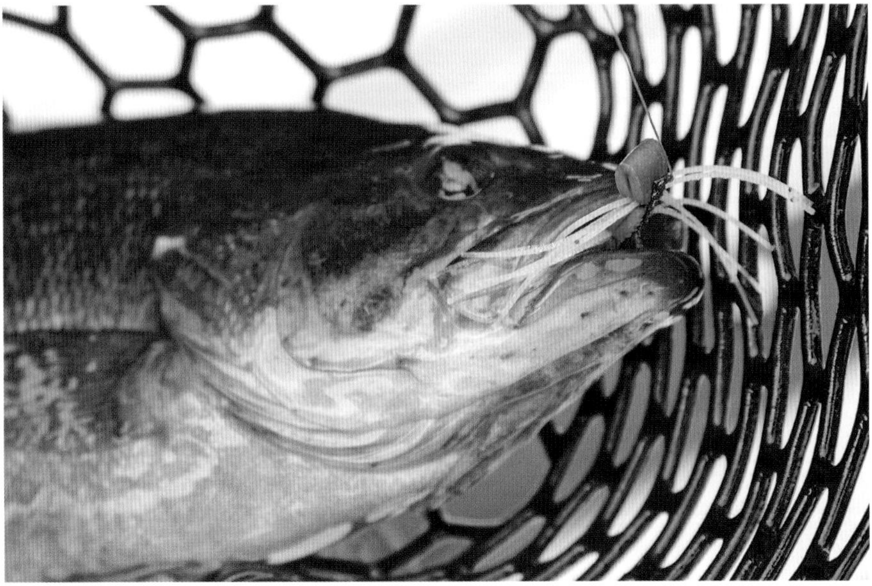

Since bass are usually more opportunistic than selective, it's possible to get by with a handful of patterns in different colors. This fish was feeding on damselflies on a shallow flat, but it eventually succumbed to an impressionistic wiggly pattern that was the same hue as its prey. Carrying wigglies in a few different sizes and colors may be all the hatch-matching you need on your local smallmouth river. That said, on slower, clearer, spring creek–like water, you might have to defer to more realistic imitations. NATE SIPPLE

Fish and anglers regard the surface differently. Fly manipulation that might seem too subtle to an angler at distance might be even too much for a bass just a few feet away. By keeping your homo-centrism in check and respecting the refined sensory organs of the bass, you'll see your topwater catch rates begin to increase. NATE SIPPLE

of angler and angled, danger and opportunity, are what make surface fishing so dynamic, interesting, and rewarding.

So we've established that the surface is a mystical barrier freighted with great significance for a fish. But it also just happens to be a key part of the echo chamber of a river. One way to think about the surface of the water is that it's the skin of a drum, a percussive instrument. The sound something makes falling onto the surface of the water and moving across the tight skin of the river is significantly different from the sound something makes falling through the water column or moving deep below the surface. And so we've classified topwater flies according to the sound they make. All of the topwater flies discussed in this chapter have a different timbre. In fact, you might think of them as musical instruments producing a variety of different sounds, from the pianissimo of the wiggly to the fortissimo of a banging Boogle Bug to the deep sonic baritone of a hair bug trapping tremendous quantities of air in its spun body. In short, more so than profile, what distinguishes the families of our four primary categories is their sonic profile.

For topwater purposes, we'll divide topwater flies into three basic categories: wigglies, poppers and sliders, and imitative insect representations. Wigglies, poppers, and sliders are used as all-around prospecting flies, whereas the imitative insect representations are used in special circumstances.

Before we start with a discussion of different topwater flies and the sounds they make, let's put our homocentrism in check and acknowledge that what the angler and the bass might call the "right amount" of sound are two different things. As a rule, people tend to fish topwater flies too aggressively: They land them too aggressively and they work them too aggressively. There's a reason for this, of course: We humans can't hear what's going on below the surface, and furthermore we're a good distance away from that casted fly we're retrieving. But what seems to us to be a minor surface disturbance might in fact be gross overstimulation for a bass. You might have heard the sound a frog makes when leaping into the water—but when was the last time you heard a frog kick? Or a dying minnow twitch?

Working a fly with too much aggression on the surface comes from the angler's fear that the fly is not getting noticed. Most of the time this idea that the fish does not perceive our fly is preposterous. If anything, the fly is usually being *too* much noticed. We can't count all the times fish have eaten with no other coaxing than the landing of the fly. As such the first rule of fishing topwaters for smallmouth is to practice patience and restraint: When the fly hits the water you have to let it marinate until the rings subside. Smallmouth know it's there. If you are the type of angler who has a hard time leaving a surface bug alone, keep telling yourself over and over: The bass's world is not our world.

Reading the Mood of Topwater Fish

Nowhere does the mood of a fish become more apparent than in fishing topwaters. We have a hard time knowing whether the fish on the end of the line took our crayfish with gusto or with hesitation, but when it comes to surface eats, a fish's attitude is plain as day. One thing we've noticed over the decades of watching smallmouth eat topwater flies is that the eats tend to come in two categories, which we call confidence eats and reactionary eats. Confidence eats are subtle but deliberate sips. Reactionary eats are more explosive. The difference between the two is not just academic.

That's because the way fish eat will tell you what kind of day you might be in for. If you see fish blowing up on poppers, don't be sold on the day just yet. Those are simply reactionary eats, and they are not a reason to put away the streamer rods just yet. It's only when you start getting sippers—confidence eats—that you can affirm that fish are comfortable feeding on the surface that day and rig all of your rods with topwaters. While both reactionary eats and confidence eats can be good and exciting, a morning that begins with several confidence eats is definitely a day where you want to be on the water.

Rubber legs give the angler the opportunity to impart meaningful action to a surface bug without really moving the fly. Most anglers are adept at noisemaking with poppers but are less skilled when it comes to the finesse movements that wigglies require. For your upcoming fishing season, work on moving your flies deliberately, but subtly. NATE SIPPLE

Where and Why to Fish Topwaters

There are two very good reasons for throwing topwater flies. One is when smallmouth don't have much water covering their backs—when they're feeding shallow by choice or when the water is low in late summer. Another consideration is the structural orientation of the smallmouth river or stretch of river you happen to be fishing. More so than anything else, a topwater fly allows you to truly saturate the y-axis river beats we discussed in the previous chapter. So if, say, you're fishing the first shelf on a long, straight stretch of river, you couldn't pick a better fly than a topwater: You'll be able to fish your fly in the most productive zone much longer than any other presentation.

The easiest, which is to say least technical, time to fish topwaters is when there's enough cfs above the first shelf for the fish to feel comfortable there. They aren't as scared as they might be in lower water, so there are a lot of flies that can work in this sort of situation. The river is low enough that you can get away with fishing terrestrials when it's calm, but high enough that you can throw poppers, even big poppers, in certain areas. There's a lot of freedom when the water is at this level, as well as room for mistakes: You can make bad casts and still get into fish.

That said, perfect water conditions are rare, so most of the time there's going to be a best possible topwater fly to throw on any given day. Let's look at the surface family of flies, starting with wigglies.

Wigglies

To tell the story of the wiggly we first have to tell the story of an elderly Southern gentleman by the name of Jack Allen. Jack was a longtime largemouth bass guide from the Florida Everglades, and when we met him at the boat launch one early summer day, we saw nothing more than a guy with a bad elbow and a box of tiny hand-tied flies with foam bodies and wiggly legs—"bluegill spiders on steroids," we called them. Little did we know that this gentleman would become a yearly customer and revolutionize the way we approached bass for the next fifteen years.

When we launched the boat that first day with Jack the winds were ripping the flags straight out and there were standing waves and whitecaps on the river—not the sort of conditions in which any of the guides would have suggested throwing something as small and delicate as one of Jack's foam and rubber creations. But there was no dissuading the old Floridian. Armed with a four-weight rod and a seven-weight line, his modus was making short, elegant casts and then letting his foam bug ride, and giving it a mend every now and again. "I like buggin'," he would affirm every couple of minutes in his trademark Southern drawl, smiling as he spoke. Every now and again he'd give his fly a wiggle or a twitch—or at least we thought he did. In the standing

The man with the plan, Jack Allen, shows off his box of small poppers and wigglies. Allen's passion for "bugging" opened up a whole new world of topwater fishing for the team at Tight Lines. NATE SIPPLE

When fishing wigglies, all subtlety ends when the fish eats. Year in and year out, small topwater flies take some of the biggest fish of the season, as Todd Polacek (bottom) and Tom Shockley (top) know all too well. ERIC CHRISTENSEN

waves and whitecaps, it would have been hard to spot a big bright blockhead popper, let alone a small dark bluegill fly, jacked up on steroids or not.

Then Jack caught a nineteen-inch fish.

And another.

The third fish we netted was a solid twenty inches. After we released it Jack flopped back down, wincing and rubbing his casting elbow. While our predominant emotion was a kind of shock at the unlikely success he'd just had, Jack's primary emotion was pain. Shaking out his elbow and getting back in the casting perch, he clarified to both us and the fish: "I prefer the fourteen-inchers."

Just like that, the wiggly revolution had begun.

In a way, fishing wigglies is not something entirely new. As far back as the 1880s, Dr. Henshall was imploring the smallmouth angler "not to forget the spiders." But as we started fishing wigglies systematically, we noticed different behaviors and even different personalities in the bass that we'd been catching for decades on poppers and hair bugs. For one, there was a difference between the eats we got on the wiggly and the eats we got on the popper. Oftentimes the popper eat is something more aggressive, a toilet bowl *woosh* or topwater explosion of sorts—all suggestive of the fact that the fish could be scared or confused or both when they take a whack at a popping bug. But wiggly fish were a different story. There was never unnecessary commotion in the eat. It was never an explosive splash. A full ten times out of ten, a smallmouth bass simply sipped it out of the film. They were confident it was food.

The importance of fishing small flies was further reinforced to us by shop-friend Dave Whitlock. Tim remembers having lunch with Dave and his wife, Emily, on the river one day when Dave picked up his rod and headed to a backwater area to make a few casts. In no time at all Dave was fast into a big fish that he brought to hand expertly. After he released the fish, Dave waded into the river toward the foam line, cupped his hand and seined the foam between his fingers. What was left in the palm of his hand was a combination of dead damselflies, dragonfly shucks, mayflies, and a host of other delicious tidbits for smallmouth. Dave smiled at us and said, "That, my friend, is why the little stuff works."

Though the above anecdotes demonstrate a fish's willingness to eat the wiggly in a variety of weather conditions and forage situations, the real problem the wiggly solves is presenting to fish in shallow, calm water. This might refer to 1) the first shelf when there is "just enough" water to bring fish onto it, 2) shallow feeding flats in the evening, and 3) mid-river rock gardens and weed beds in the middle of the day. For these reasons the wiggly typically becomes an especially important fly in the smallmouth angler's arsenal once water levels drop a bit in early summer.

Fishing the Wiggly

First things first. The wiggly is not a popping bug, so the most important rule to remember when fishing one is simple: Don't pop it. That's because the power of the wiggly lies in its seductive subtlety—aka, the wiggle—which goes out the window when you yank it across the surface. Having fished these flies with hundreds of clients, we've settled on a single verbal instruction that accurately communicates how subtle of a motion the fishing of these flies requires: "Bend its legs. Don't move the bug, just bend its legs." How much line manipulation is needed to bend legs made of one-millimeter silicone? Not much. But it's a fact: When fishing a wiggly, less is truly more.

Aside from a less-is-more approach to the wiggly's action, the topwater angler has a responsibility to think through the path, aka the drift, of the fly. Landing the fly to make sure it travels along meaningful structure is key, and mending to either reposition or extend the drift—in other words, to keep it on the water and in the zone as much as possible—is a big part of successful

Right to left from top: Chernobyl Ant (black and tan), Damsel Wiggly/Charlie Piette, Dragon Wiggly/Charlie Piette, Ol' Mr. Wiggly (tan)/Charlie Piette, Whitlock's Crystal Dragonfly/Dave Whitlock, South Fork Chernobyl, Chernobyl Ant (black and chartreuse), Fat Albert/Brent Taylor, Ol' Mr. Wiggly (yellow)/Charlie Piette. DAVE KARCZYNSKI

wiggly fishing. This might mean making sure that the fly is drifting along y-axis structure like shelf edges. Or that, when targeting apertures in the weeds, it actually floats over, and not to the side of, the holes bass use to ambush their prey. Charlie had the perfect example of this one day with a husband-and-wife team one day in late July.

The husband was an experienced angler and good caster and fished in the back of the boat all day. He was fishing a neutrally buoyant baitfish and was doing just okay. His wife was fishing a wiggly, but she was newer to casting and still working on gaining distance (her average casts at the time were probably in the twenty- to twenty-five-foot range). But what she lacked in the distance game, she made up for in how she fished the wiggly she was throwing. She thoroughly understood the importance of getting the fly at the appropriate angle out in front of the boat and then mending her line to achieve a perfect dead-drift. Charlie's job was to make sure the boat was positioned at casting distance to the shelf edges. Though she never imparted any motion to the bug

Got your sights on a large fish cruising in shallow water? Delivering a wiggly at distance with a delicate tuck cast and then bending the legs of the fly as a fish inspects the offering is a sure way to a bent rod. MICHAEL LESCHISIN

the entire day, she just cleaned house, with fish happily rising out of relatively deep water to eat the dead-drifted wiggly all day. For anglers accustomed to micromanaging the actions of their streamers, fishing the wiggly can require a Zen-like patience and detachment. When you were first learning to fly cast, you probably heard your teacher say over and over, "Let the rod do the work." A somewhat similar lesson applies to the wiggly: "Let the fly do the work."

The true wiggly artist will master mending in such a way that breathes life into the legs. Try to accomplish a "touch" mend, where you exaggerate your mend slightly to come into contact with the fly—the exact opposite of what you'd be looking to do when dry-fly fishing for trout.

Poppers

Before we get started about poppers, which have been around in either deer hair, balsa wood, or foam forms since time immemorial, it might be worth asking an obvious question: Why on earth does a smallmouth bass eat a chartreuse popper in the first place? Our years on the water have led us to believe that a big part of the reason that smallmouth eat things like gaudy fluorescent poppers is due to the "curse of no opposable thumbs." When a human being finds something interesting, we use our hands to grasp it and

Top to bottom, left to right: Porky's Pet/Dave Whitlock, Boogle Bug/Boogle Bug, Express Bug/Chuck Kraft, Fruit Cocktail/Dave Whitlock, Amnesia Bug/Boogle Bug, XCalibur Bug/Chuck Kraft, Blockhead Popper/Tim Holschlag, Boogle Bullet/Boogle Bug, CKadia/Chuck Kraft, Big Pop/Rainy's Flies, Umpqua Bass Popper (frog)/Umpqua Feather Merchants, CKadia Round/Chuck Kraft, Umpqua Bass Popper (minnow)/Umpqua Feather Merchants, Walt's Popper/Walt Cary, Boga/Chuck Kraft. DAVE KARCZYNSKI

pull it close to get a better look. But bass, along with all species of game fish, unfortunately lack that resource. If you put something interesting into the "zone," a bass becomes immediately concerned with whether or not the new object is food. Of course, determining this requires the bass to put the item in question into its mouth—and you know what happens next. Bass, and especially river bass, need to feed all day long in order to survive, and with the abundance of opportunities floating past all season long, a fish must check out unusual foodstuffs from time to time in order to keep building calories. We have seen bass sip a spindly leaf with the same confidence as they would an adult dragonfly, only to kick it out once they recognize the mistake. The actionable difference is that the mistakes we throw their way have a hook at the end of them.

Any modern conversation about popping bugs should probably begin with the Boogle Bug. One of the most commonly deployed smallmouth flies throughout the country, a whole cult of awe has surrounded the mighty Boogle family of flies. There are Boogle Bug T-shirts, Boogle Bug stickers, even Boogle Bug Internet memes. The thing that distinguishes the Boogle Bug from other poppers is the variety and vividness of its paint job, which also accounts for the longevity of the fly. Boogles have such a hard, sturdy layer of shellack that they feel—and fish—like balsa poppers. This means that they can achieve high line speeds, which means that you can land them hard if you need to—say, when fishing stained water or when you need to call a fish up from the depths. Remember that half of a topwater fly's sonic profile is how it lands. It's a fact that a Boogle Bug coming down probably makes the sharpest sound of the topwater flies discussed in this chapter. Whether hitting the water softly or quickly, the Boogle makes a crisp, sharp sound when it lands.

Untreated foam, on the other hand, creates a bit of friction that slows the fly down in the air and reduces the surface area coming into contact with the water on the cast. All things being equal, these flies will land a bit more softly. And the softest landers, at least before they become waterlogged, are hair bugs, since the texture of the spun, trimmed deer hair catches quite a bit of air as it is cast.

We'll begin our popper conversation talking about concave head poppers, which are by far the most common type of popper. We'll then move on to flat-faced poppers and sliders.

When and How to Pop

If there's a basic recipe for popper fishing, one that we might tweak based on the conditions at hand, it's this:

1. Land the fly as gently as you can. The sound of the fly hitting the water is the first possible cue to bring a fish in.
2. Let the bug drift at least until the rings of water clear. Or longer (because less is more, longer is better).
3. Mend if need be.
4. Let the rings of water clear again.
5. Repeat.

With that basic recipe established, there are several other factors that affect the way we fish popping bugs. The first is the depth of the water. The key with any popping bug is as follows: Shallow water gets a little pop, deep water gets a big pop. Deeper water, as a rule, asks for greater sound: a louder landing on the cast and a more resonant pop on the retrieve. In x-axis situations where you are fishing a popper all the way back to the boat over water steadily

One great thing about smallmouth bass is that you rarely need to wake up early or stay late to experience good fishing. A bass's willingness to eat throughout any old sunny afternoon is just one more thing that makes it such a gift to anglers. KYLE ZEMPEL

increasing depth, this means that the intensity of pops should increase steadily as the fly approaches deeper water.

A quick word about when to make the first pop: Many anglers will cast a popper and pop it the moment after it lands, thinking they have just imparted the "first" pop. In fact, this is the second pop—the moment when the popper hits the water is the first pop. This is an important distinction to make because many times a smallmouth will immediately swim over to a fly after it lands, finning downstream with the fly just a few inches from its nose as it tries to decide whether to eat or not. A premature second pop oftentimes spooks away a fish that was probably just going to eat your fly anyways. When the popper hits the right water and drifts along, it is fishing . . . period. We have had countless anglers lose track of their poppers as they offer a story or joke, and after what seems like an eternity, somewhere in midsentence, we will hear a loud slurp. Food does not always have to be banging away at the surface to get noticed. Next time you're on the river fishing topwaters, play a game with yourself where you try to stew the fly as long as possible. We think you'll be pleased with the results.

While small pops in deeper water will still take fish, the same is not true in the inverse. Big pops in skinny water are the smallmouth equivalent of a HazMat sign. It's just too, too much. Sometimes against our expressed wishes, we'll have a client make a big pop in shallow water—and then we'll shake our heads at all the "V" wakes shooting away. We work tremendously hard to get our clients to practice restraint with their poppers on late summer water. How hard, you ask? After hearing our "let it stew" spiel for the tenth time over the

Poppers will make different sounds on landing depending on their core body materials and level of dressing. A minimalist foam-head popper (far left) can be cast with great line speed for a sharp sound upon landing, whereas a spun-deer-hair body with plenty of hackles and rubber legs (middle) will invariably land more softly. DAVE KARCZYNSKI

Guide Charlie Piette watches his client's popper for signs of an approaching fish. Popping to "call fish up" and popping to "seal the deal" are two different things. Sharper, louder pops garner a fish's attention, but the same pop performed with a bass just inches from the fly is more likely to scare it away. At such times, a gentle motion gets the eat. Of course, the only way to know which pop the situation calls for is to have a firm visual understanding of the scene. NATE SIPPLE

course of a fishing day, we actually had a client turn to us and say, "You know you really should call them 'sitters,' not 'poppers.'"

In addition to depth, temperature is another important factor that affects our approach to popping. Cool-water popping and warmer-water popping should be approached differently in terms of attitude and expectation. Early in the season when bass metabolic rates are slow, you might get hit eight seconds into the drift because that's how long it takes for that lethargic fish to move from his lie to your fly. That's a time to stay focused on the fly throughout the drift, and not to lose your attention even after the fly has been sitting out there for some time. Later in the season, when bass metabolic rates are at their peak, the angler must be ready for the opposite: an instantaneous eat. When water temps are high, you don't want to be adjusting your sunglasses or unwrapping a line from around your reel seat when the fly lands. You want to be ready to strike.

Given the importance of visual strike detection when it comes to fishing topwaters, it pays to know what visuals to expect of surface eats as well. During pre-spawn, for instance, the popper eat is completely different from what it will look like during the summer months. At this early point in the season, fish will roll up slowly on the fly. Oftentimes you will see the dark bronze of the fish approaching—and the next thing you know, your popper has disappeared. By the time water temps reach into the mid-sixties, however, the taxonomy of eats expands to include the more water-shattering implosions and explosions—the most exciting eats of the season, in other words.

So depth and temperature of the water are two things that we take into account when determining the intensity of our approach, but in clear water when we can see our quarry there's another dimension the thoughtful topwater angler must think about: the proximity of the fish. In clear water where you can see fish, use the distance of a fish to determine how hard of a pop to employ. The closer the fish, the quieter the pop. This of course goes back to the sonic element of the fly. With a fish at distance you might have needed to shout to get his attention, but you don't want to keep shouting after you have his ear. In many cases, the fish will charge the fly and eat it after a single pop. But then there are other times when a fish will charge toward a fly several yards away and not eat but pause beneath it, laid up beneath your bug like a seal with a ball on its nose. In such circumstances, if you give your fly a normal pop, that bass will be gone. At times like this it's a whisper, not a shout, that will seal the deal. This means moving your fly the absolute most minimal amount. With a fish looking at your fly cross-eyed, your job as the angler is not to pop the bug but, as in the case of the wiggly, to try to bend its legs (or wiggle its tail if it doesn't have legs).

In murkier water, or when fishing at a distance, sometimes you won't actually see the fish studying your fly, but there are other indications that a fish is directly beneath—the bug may heave a bit on the surface of the water, or you might see a nervous shimmer directly beneath the bug. In any case, the situation is the same: Make your fly whisper, not shout. Rubber legs are great whispering tools since they give you the opportunity to impart subtle action to a popping bug without popping it.

The next style of popper we'll look at is the flat-faced blockhead popper, which is probably the easiest shape for the at-home foam cutter to create. Blockhead poppers are less streamlined than Boogle Bugs, and, as we've mentioned earlier, the untreated foam creates a little more friction with the air. All this comes together to create a slightly softer landing on the surface—not nearly as soft as a wiggly, of course, but also not as sharp as a Boogle Bug. That said, the most salient feature of the blockhead is its oversized flat head—a musical instrument capable of the loudest surface noise among the popper family. Try giving one of these flies a long sharp pop and you'll see—and hear—what we mean. We will fish these flies on deeper water shelves or when we need a mid-river noisemaker. When fish are looking at topwaters and you want to pop deeper water, the blockhead is your friend—it can really call fish

Topwater flies are certainly not only for fishing the first shelf or overt cover. Fish sitting in mid-river weeds and rock gardens are also highly susceptible to well-presented poppers and wigglies. NATE SIPPLE

up from the deep. Just don't pop one aggressively on a skinny flat. You will quickly find yourself the only predator in sight.

There are other situations that call for a soft landing with the ability to make significant sound. Say you're fishing a short, shallow shelf that drops off suddenly into deeper water. You might want to be delicate at the beginning of your casts (you're landing in very shallow water) but noisy toward the end (because the water drops off to mid-depth fairly quickly and you need sound to grab a fish's attention). In this case, blockhead poppers popped with increasing aggression as the water deepens are the way to go.

That all being said, fish behavior varies by region and watershed, and the fish in your system may respond somewhat differently to poppers—indeed, the variability in bass response to topwaters is one of the things that makes smallmouth fishing so fascinating. Our observations have led us to believe that the farther east one goes, the more likely bass are to pursue topwaters fished more aggressively. We have friends and clients in the Mid-Atlantic region who are very experienced smallmouth anglers, and they swear that more movement is better on their home waters. Trial, error, and success will tell you the topwater preferences for smallmouth on your watershed on a given day, month, or year.

Sliders

Sliders are another family of topwater fly. With the tapered, bullet-like head of a slider, our presentation tips more toward movement and away from sound. Throw a slider in the water and you'll see that the trade-off is clear: You are only able to accomplish more movement because you are generating less sonic commotion.

Sliders are a good choice when you want to not just drift but move a topwater fly in skinny water. Take the following scenario: You want to fish a topwater fly, but you are looking at x-axis river structure where fish are holding in lies that are perpendicular to shore or path of the boat—for instance, large submerged trees jutting out from the bank into the river channel. Whereas the slower Boogle Bug or wiggly will allow you to fish on the surface alongside part of the tree, a slider that can be worked quicker without causing too much surface disturbance will allow you to cover more of the length of the tree. On truly slow water, you may be able to fish the full length of the perpendicular structure.

The other advantage that sliders have over other, slower topwater baits is that they can be manipulated in different ways to convert neutral but curious fish into striking. Sliders are the one true topwater fly where it's possible to make it look like it's trying to flee. Try to create a "fleeing" motion with a popper and you'll end up kicking a tremendous amount of wake and will almost certainly put a fish down; this is why we encouraged you in the previous section to focus on simply bending the legs of the fly. But a slider can be twitched to make it look like it is trying to get away. Thus, sliders can be a tool to solve the problem of curious but moody fish that are inspecting popping bugs and wigglies but not committing. At times like this, a fish might need to give chase to get excited.

Whether you're fishing wigglies, poppers, or sliders, one essential element of successful topwater fishing is to learn to focus your vision not at the fly but around it. Clients are constantly amazed when their guide calmly instructs them to "leave it, wait . . . wait, now just bend the legs," and magically an otherwise invisible nineteen-inch bass confidently sips the offering. The client never saw the fish because he had a laser-like focus on the fly. This is understandable: Bass flies are cool looking and usually easy to see. But laser vision just doesn't cut it in smallmouth fishing. Their guide, if he or she is worth their salt, has learned the fine art of multitasking vision between the bug and the water underneath it. Train your eyes to focus more on a hula hoop–size area around the fly, and you too will see more fish and learn how to read their mood, or at the very least not rip a fly away from a fish that is looking to eat.

Topwater Lines

Imagine the following situation: You've just cast a topwater fifty feet, and no sooner has your fly landed than you see a fish boil fifteen yards downstream. You need to pick your fly up at distance and immediately put it back down again in the vicinity of the boil. Problem is, you're fishing a shooting-head line with a very aggressive weight-forward taper. To prepare for the next cast, you must strip the line back in twenty-five to thirty feet to get to the castable part of the head. But now, your target fish is long gone. You've wasted a lot of energy for nothing. Do this sort of thing all day long, and you're experiencing a significant reduction in the amount of time your fly actually spends on the water.

While aggressive weight-forward shooting heads have a place in smallmouth fishing, for topwater fishing we favor the ability to aerialize line, manipulate it with in-air mends, reposition the fly once it has landed, lift it off the water at great distances, and use surgical mending (aka touch mending) to bend the legs of the fly. The sort of topwater line we favor for these applications has the line's mass distributed fairly evenly throughout head and body of the line

Conventionally tapered lines with an extant rear belly allow for loop control at great distance. They are the most versatile of topwater lines. MICHAEL LESCHISIN

and also possesses a gentle rear taper. A gentle rear taper gives you the ability to fish poppers or wigglies at a distance, since you can pick up and put down flies with a single back-cast.

Another thing we like about lines with a rear taper is that they can be mended more easily at distance. When fishing topwaters, you are going to be casting over faster water toward slower water, regardless of whether you are fishing in a boat or standing midstream in current. The most common topwater presentation begins with an upstream reach cast followed by a long-distance stack mend once the fly hits the water.

In short, the best topwater lines we have found tend to be the more aggressive trout tapers—Airflo Exceed, Rio Grand, RIO Gold, and Scientific Angler GPX and MPX tapers all fit the bill. They are weight forward enough to turn flies over but also possess all the other elements necessary to fish topwaters successfully day in and day out.

The large weight-forward shooting heads that have garnered much of the marketing attention in recent years can have a place even in the topwater game, but you will gain much more versatility and accuracy out of a more traditional line, even as ease of turning the fly over is compromised. With the mega-oversize lines, you minimize your accuracy no matter how good the caster's form and technique. They are not designed for the surgical style of fishing that is often needed topwater hunting on shallow flats.

TOPWATER CASTS

Casting poppers requires high line speeds to overcome their inherent air resistance. Single and double hauls become important not only to gain distance but also to unfurl the leader appropriately. If you are having a difficult time turning over your fly, spend some time working closer in, and then working out a few feet at a time.

Once you feel comfortable with your casting distance, it's time to think about the angle of the cast. When fishing topwaters from a moving boat, one thing we repeat over and over to our clients is this: "Don't fish in the past." One of the guides' biggest pet peeves is when anglers cast directly across to the banks: Not only are you casting to fish that have already seen the boat, but you are courting drag. Ideally, you should aspire to show any given bass your bug before you or the boat reaches its field of vision. Part of fishing consistently in the future means keeping your cast out in front of you as you dead-drift a bug downstream.

Fished from a boat, topwater flies are most effectively presented with a straight-line connection between the fly rod and the fly—a bowed line creates presentation and hook set problems. But whether you're standing midstream or floating in a boat, you will almost always be dealing with multiple current

Even fish lurking on the bottom of a flat have a good idea of what's going on at the surface. Less is often much, much more when it comes to fishing topwaters for smallmouth. ERIC CHRISTENSEN

seams—especially when fishing the first shelf. The water near the bank will indeed be slower than the water between you and the shelf, even if you are moving downstream with the boat. Throw a standard cast onto that water and you'll immediately notice a bow in the line. To solve this problem, one common topwater cast we use is the reach cast, which is simply an aerial mend you accomplish by moving your rod tip in an upstream direction while your line is shooting. A reach cast starts you off on the right foot with your topwater drift.

The tuck cast is another important topwater cast used in the case of extreme low water when we want the softest presentation possible. A tuck cast is where we stop our rod tip early and let the line and leader straighten out a few feet above the water instead of on the water. The idea is that instead of whipping onto the surface of the water, the fly and leader slowly drops to the surface on a soft slack line. The soft landing aids in convincing the bass that this freshly fallen food is not dangerous, only delicious.

Be it in the form of special casts or mends, line management is crucial when fishing topwaters for smallmouth because bass rarely eat surface bugs on the swing. They do, however, eat divers on the swing. So if the surface bite is on but you or your fishing partner are having trouble with line control, a diver might just be more your style. We'll talk more about divers to kick off the next chapter.

The Topwater Hook Set and Battle

The best hook set when fishing topwaters is not a strip set or side-sweep. Instead, you should come straight up with the rod and at the same time make one long, strong strip until the rod has a good bend in it. Setting straight up and with a strip when fishing topwaters is tremendously important toward achieving consistent quality hook sets. That said, setting to the side can also work if the rod set follows the current in a downstream direction, but unless you know which direction the fish ate the fly from, a low side set runs the risk of pulling the fly out of a fish's mouth.

So you've made a careful presentation, goaded a fish into eating, and stuck him clean. Now, the fight is on. With any popping bugs or wigglies, if we lose a fish it is usually within the first three seconds. Even if it's on the second, deeper shelf, a fish typically eats and heads for even deeper water—right at you, in other words. It can be very hard to catch up to these charging fish. What we tell our clients is this: "Strip aggressively as if you were trying to break the fish off—until you come tight to them again." This command puts into their heads that they have to be aggressive with the fish to make up all that slack line that a charging fish introduces. Practice making a stripping motion

Littoral areas can also make for exciting topwater fishing. When calling fish up from deeper water, look to blockhead poppers with a flat face. A big initial pop followed by long pauses and smaller movements is a good approach for fishing still water. LUKE KAVAJECZ

that is large and all the way past your belt line. We watch anglers continually use great effort making a dozen small strips when one or two giant strips will be far more effective. Oftentimes an angler might stop stripping because they think the fish is gone. Don't. Keep stripping with the biggest, longest strips you can muster. Odds are that bass is still there.

How to Approach Feeding Flats

Much of our topwater fishing occurs on shallow feeding flats. One bit of advice that's been passed on to us from Larry Mann of the Hayward Fly Fishing Company, and which we now pass on to you, is this: "Don't crowd the kitchen." Keep your boat or person as far away from the flat as possible, and only work your way in slowly after you have thoroughly fished the area. The problem with working in too close to a feeding flat is that you may spook fish, which in turn may spook other fish, starting a chain reaction that will soon leave your busy flat totally devoid of smallmouth life.

FISHING TOPWATERS FROM A MOVING BOAT VS. WADING

Because smallmouth rivers tend to be a bit larger and deeper than trout streams, anglers are often confronted with the question of whether to fish from a boat or wade. It's really a personal preference—we have many clients who love to wade fish, even as we move them from spot to spot in the drift boat. They love the feel of the water and the intimate relationship with the slow and subtle approach. We also have anglers that will fish only out of a boat. They need to cover water and constantly be moving. Neither is right or wrong. Let's take a look at the pros and cons of each approach when it comes to fishing topwaters.

First off, boat fishing has many advantages. Fishing topwaters from a moving boat allows for the longest drag-free drifts and also makes available the maximum topwater "moves"—twitches, wiggles, pops, touch mends, and so on, with relative ease (if you've ever tried to fish a popper properly while wading in heavy flows, you know what we're talking about). But making consistently successful topwater presentations from a moving boat also takes thought, vision, and planning. In order to be successful, you must set yourself up for success, and part of that success comes from recognizing that there's a best way to fish each spot, and that you are only going to get one chance to fish it. Miss your target or make a sloppy cast and it's over. Casting angles are also more limited in a boat, especially with two anglers in the boat. Casting at a forty-five-degree angle downstream allows for good drifts and cuts down on midair line collisions.

Wading offers one big advantage: the ability to work one area incredibly thoroughly and from both upstream and downstream positions. That said, care should be taken when choosing presentation positions. While not always as spooky as a trout, smallmouth can be lined and spooked. Aspire to up-and-across or down-and-across presentations when fishing topwaters to smallmouth from wading positions. Especially if you intend to make multiple presentations, take pains not to float your line over potential fish. One thing to keep in mind is that the ability for wading anglers to fish effectively on the surface becomes more difficult as flows increase. In heavy water it becomes very hard to get a dead drift, and even more difficult to pop or twitch the fly without creating drag. In such cases, divers, which we discuss in the next chapter, tend to be a better option if you want to fish right near the surface. The fact that you can swim them crosscurrent makes them easier to fish appropriately.

Skating Flies for Smallmouth

Former Scientific Angler line designer Andrew Bosway has developed a unique system for targeting smallmouth on small to midsize rivers: skating topwaters. His success with this technique on the rivers of Michigan and Indiana confirm that there are indeed exceptions to the idea that smallmouth almost always eat on the pause, largely because, when skating flies, there is no pause (though with some subtle rod manipulations you can indeed pulse the fly).

This technique is most satisfying to fish with a six- or seven-weight switch rod coupled with a Skagit head of a grain weight appropriate for the rod's action and the caster's style. While a Scandi head also works, a Skagit allows you to switch between skating a dry and swinging a weighted fly with great ease: Simply remove the floating tip and replace it with a poly leader or even a long, tapered mono leader and voilá—you've gone from fishing shallow to deep. Of course, you can also skate flies with a single-handed rod if you so please.

Skating flies has a time and place, but it is certainly not all times and it is not every place. This technique works best on small to midsize rivers where it's possible to cover most, if not all, of the river in a single swing. That's because skating flies requires "players" to work, and players of the type that chase skated flies can be few and far between. In this sense, skating flies is similar to fishing large, flashy streamers from a boat in an attempt to elicit territorial strikes. In both cases you are covering a lot of water, accepting that passive and

Skating surface flies allows the wading angler to cover water quickly and efficiently. It's the closest thing to fishing from a boat when you're without one. Skating flies works best when when water temps are warm and bass metabolism is high. KYLE ZEMPEL

Successful surface skating is less about which fly is being used and more about the wake that a given fly creates. Tinker with the angle and speed of your fly until you achieve a wake about the size of a slice of pizza. ERIC CHRISTENSEN

neutral fish are going to ignore your offering but feeling confident that you're covering enough water efficiently enough to entice aggressive fish into eating.

Fly size factors into the casting more than the fishing. Because this technique is most successful when you can cover significant water, you need a fly that can be cast a considerable distance with relative ease. Small foam terrestrial patterns in the size six neighborhood are ideal. Remember that the overall impression of the bug will seem larger given the fact that it is creating a wake on the surface. What about mice, you might ask? While smallmouth do indeed chase mouse patterns during the daylight hours, we've found that mice are difficult to cast a long distance with a switch rod, and it's really the length of the cast and the speed of the skate—and not the fly itself—that seems to be the determining factor in the success of this technique.

There are two important components to this technique, the first and most important being the length of the cast, the second being the speed of the skate. First let's deal with the length of the cast. As mentioned above, this technique works because not every smallmouth in the river is going to give chase to a skated bug. Indeed, it's only the most aggressive fish on any given day that are going to give chase. Thus the skated-fly approach is most successful when you can cover most of the river in a single cast. If you can stand on the first shelf of one bank, cast to the first shelf of the far bank, and skate across the entire length of the river, you have found yourself skatable water. Using this technique, it is quite possible to present to every single fish in a given beat of water.

The second important part of this technique is the speed of the fly. Too slow and fish have too much time to think—we want them to simply respond. Too fast, on the other hand, and it just doesn't feel like food. So how do you know the right speed? One way to think about speed is by the size of your wake. When skating flies for smallmouth, you should aspire to a wake that is about the size of a slice of pizza. A too-fast retrieve will create too large a wake, a too-slow retrieve generally too small. Aim for a healthy pizza slice, and you're on your way to garnering reaction strikes up top.

Skating flies for smallmouth can be an excellent way to explore new water, since you'll identify those locations in a beat of river where the most active fish reside. One idea for incorporating skating into your repertoire is to spend the morning skating a topwater over several hundred yards of river, then return to your point of entry and swing a leech. Doing so will cue you in on location and habits of the fish in your river and is an easy way to expedite the wading angler's understanding of new water.

Andrew Bosway and canine smallmouth whisperer Finn trudge out into a shallow river to begin skating flies. Expert spey casters may find it possible to launch their flies from one bank to the other, but for single-handed rods and more casual casting, try standing in the middle of the river and casting to either bank before moving a few yards downstream and repeating. DAVE HOSLER

Aquatic Insects

We're saving a discussion for aquatic insects for the end of this chapter—mostly because fishing imitative representations of flies in hatch-matching contexts presents a smaller window of opportunity than fishing more impressionistic offerings like wigglies, poppers, and sliders as search patterns. That said, there are times when imitative representations can be quite important. The smallmouth's relationship to aquatic insects is emblematic of its relationship to preystuffs in general: The more prolific the preystuff, the more important it is to the smallmouth bass.

Because the sport emerged from beneath the wide cloak of trout fishing, smallmouth fishing with a fly rod began largely as a hatch-matching enterprise. And while the sport has evolved considerably since then, aquatic insects still occupy a place of importance in the diet of the smallmouth bass and in the methodology of the bass angler. That said, it's worth reaffirming here that bass are not trout. Bass orient and respond to aquatic insects differently than trout do. We had to learn this the hard way.

One pivotal moment in our understanding of the bass in comparison to trout came years ago when Tim was fishing with longtime clients and friends Mike Rock and Bob Harrison. They ran into an amazing hatch of Hendricksons, and the smallmouth were responding to their presence with gusto. Now Mike is a fanatical trout angler and wanted to put his big box of imitations to good use. Tim pulled up to a backwater and spotted a large smallmouth feeding in a circular motion in a far corner of the pool. The subtle riseform suggested he was feeding not on the adults but on emerging insects. Of course, Mike had plenty of Hendrickson emergers tied. Tim tapered the leader down, dressed the new fly with floatant, and slowly moved the boat into position.

Mike made many beautiful presentations to the feeding fish, but to no avail. The fish kept eating but steered clear of the emerger. A trout-centric approach would have called for perhaps a different emerger pattern, or locating the fly somewhere different in the film. But Tim had a hunch and motioned to Bob, the other angler, to take the bow, handing him a rod with a small black popper. Bob cast a long line directly in line to the still-feeding smallmouth. Without any hesitation the bass tipped up and ate the popper.

More discoveries of how bass differ from trout came to us while fishing flying ant hatches. Perhaps no other food organism gets the smallmouth to the surface faster than this little insect. It usually starts with a smattering of size eighteen males on the surface that brings a few fish up. But the real magic happens when the queens begin to show up. The queen flying ants are a size fourteen, and the smaller males congregate on the abdomen of the female in

Top to bottom, left to right: Green and Blue Giant Dragonfly, Tan Giant Dragonfly, Nuvo Spider, Spent Blue Damsel, Spent Red Damsel, Dirty Olive Articulated Emerger, Dragonfly Nymph (down hook), Dragonfly Nymph (uphook), Dragonfly Nymph (Ice Dub), Dave's Bass Hopper, Dave's Cricket, Nuvo Spider. All flies designed and tied by Dave Whitlock. DAVE KARCZYNSKI

a mating ritual, creating quite a tasty clump of food. This is the moment we see exactly how many smallmouth are in the river. Bank-to-bank rings appear, and fish feed slowly and deliberately on the ants.

For years and years, we fished small rods and tiny, perfectly tied ant patterns to imitate the hatch. But what we gradually found is that instead of matching the hatch, we could be far more effective with "foody" versions of ants. Nowadays, we would much rather fish a small black- or rust-colored popper or a wiggly over an ant pattern. During ant and other emergences, we have found that taking pains to *differentiate* your bug as opposed to *imitating* the naturals will make you far more successful. For those of us who are trout anglers as well, we think: This just can't be right. But it is. We've come to understand that embedded in the smallmouth DNA is this idea that opportunity trumps quantity. Even in the heaviest hatch situations, oftentimes smallmoth bass can't help themselves.

The importance of various aquatic insects varies by watershed and region. But in general there is a hierarchy to the importance of bugs to bass. In general the quantity and duration of odanates, a family that includes dragonflies and damselflies, makes them a preferred foodstuff of smallmouth bass throughout much of the summer. Certain mayfly hatches will also draw reasonable amounts of attention. Last but not least are the terrestrials, in particular flying ants. While these insects are not around often, when they are, it is by the millions and makes for some of the most exciting fishing you could hope to encounter.

Let's take a look at smallmouth foodstuffs that benefit from imitative representations. While nowhere near as predictable as trout fishing, fishing bugs to bass is well worth trying. Keep a six weight in the boat and a handful of relevant trout-style flies at the ready.

Caddis

Of the insect species, caddis are probably the least important of the aquatic insects. For one, caddis hatches on the warm-water river stretches smallmouth inhabit tend to be sporadic—but there are exceptions. Once we were on a float and saw the water boiling with activity. The riseforms looked like trout were taking emergers—but there were no trout in this river. Fishing an olive wet fly down and across, we caught fish after fish whose mouths were bright green from gorging on caddis pupa as they ascended the water column. Fish taking caddis resemble their *trutta* counterparts in riseform: voracious subsurface swirls where they snatch the fast-moving pupa. Unlike trout fishing, however, imitations do not have to be exact: Small wet flies in bright green should suffice. Because caddis-eating smallmouth are considered a very specific situation, we advocate saving your caddis imitations for feeding fish—they shouldn't be treated as a prospecting tool.

Mayflies

When it comes to casting to rising smallmouth bass during a mayfly emergence, we have found many times that rising smallmouth bass don't hold and feed the same way trout do. A smallmouth may hang mid-river and feed over a larger range than a holding trout would. During a major hatch a smallmouth may rise once, move many feet, and rise again. We have fished hundreds of rising smallmouth and found that changing flies to more closely

When you start seeing a smattering of Hexagenia *duns, it's worth spending late nights on the water. On many Midwestern watersheds, the hex hatch provides opportunities for trophy smallmouth and brown trout, even on the same evening. But you should expect the two species to eat bugs differently. Brown trout will hold in a fixed position and rise rhythmically, whereas smallmouth will cruise around a pool and rise sporadically. Immediately covering a freshly risen smallmouth with a quick cast is the best way to make sure the right fish sees your bug.*

ERIC CHRISTENSEN

match the imitation is not usually the key to success. Much more important was "covering" the fish with the fly as soon as you see the riseform. A trout will rise from a holding lie focusing on a single insect it intends to eat, but a smallmouth is just looking for an opportunity, cruising and sipping wherever food appears. Many times a fish that has just risen to a bug will simply turn again at the sound of the landing fly and eat that as well. Smallmouth do not need to go back to the holding lie to regroup before they rise again, as do trout. On those rare occasions when we see smallmouth rising with a more trout-like consistency in a fixed feeding lane, the best approach is to cast two feet in front of the fish, allow the fly to settle, and then impart a small twitch as it comes into the strike zone. This small amount of action capitalizes on the aggressive and curious nature of the bass.

Mayfly opportunities will vary according to river and region. In general, the first important mayflies are the Hendrickson, followed by green, brown, and gray drakes. Midsummer may find you encountering one of several *Hexagenia* varieties. And as summer trends to fall, there is the white fly, *Ephoron leukon*, which in some watersheds can be so significant we will devote a separate section to them.

EPHORON LEUKON

Probably the most important mayfly to the smallmouth angler is the white fly, or *Ephoron leukon*, which emerges at the end of August. Ephorons emerge at dusk and can make for some exciting surface-fishing opportunities. On many smallmouth streams, this bug represents the biggest aquatic insect event of the season. They can emerge in such dense numbers that you've got to be careful not to open your mouth when your headlamp is on—ephorons are positively phototactic, which means they are strongly attracted to light.

Ephorons are unique among mayflies in that they complete their mating and death cycles in a single day. The males emerge shortly before the females, take to the trees, and molt into spinners in just half an hour. By the time the females emerge, they are already being accosted by males. They mate, everyone dies, and the river is blanketed with food. The emergence typically starts two hours before dusk and continues into the dark, with peak activity occurring at last light.

Smallmouth insect offerings don't need to be complicated. A few hex patterns in sizes six and eight, white mayflies in the ten- to twelve-size range, Adamses in twelve to fourteen sizes, and nymphs in sizes six to eight will cover just about everything. If you tie your own patterns, experiment with incorporating rubber legs on your dries. Smallmouth are more likely than trout to respond to a twitched bug, and those rubber legs will help seal the deal on the twitch. DAVE KARCZYNSKI

Headlamps and hex go together like peanut butter and jelly. Remember that Hexagenia *emergences are not just for rivers. Many Midwestern lakes also see significant insect emergences, and bug activity on still water usually starts before the river hatch. In addition to smallmouth, you may get the bonus walleye on a dry fly—truly a unique experience.* ERIC CHRISTENSEN

What makes a good white fly pool? While these flies emerge up and down the river corridor, spinner falls can be most dense just below riffles, as the turbulent air above a riffle acts as a kind of invisible dam. And what's the best imitation? A generic, white-hackled mayfly imitation is usually all that's needed to pique the interest of ephoron-eating smallmouth. That said, during the thickest spinner falls the biggest challenge during one of these blizzard hatches can be getting noticed. Whereas we'd try to hew closely to the naturals if we were fishing brown trout (and indeed you might find yourself casting to both at the same time during an *Ephoron* hatch if you fish transitional water), in garnering a smallmouth's attention it can be worthwhile to go up one size, since these bugs often clump and cluster, and a larger offering might give you a better chance of being noticed. When fish fail to eat, keep casting and don't get discouraged. Often it's less a refusal of your fly as an overabundance of competition.

The white fly is one bug that can really change the dynamic of a river beyond the period of the emergence. If the eddies smell like rotting carcasses and are white with crumpled bodies, odds are fish were pigging out on leukons the night before. This sometimes translates to stuffed, lethargic daytime fish. The takeaway: On rivers and at times of year when ephorons emerge in great numbers, it might make more sense to focus fishing efforts in the evening hours.

Dragonflies and Damselflies

Dragonflies and damselflies—the two most important members of the odonate family—are some of the most common insects we see flying along the river corridor on a summer day. In northern Wisconsin, we start to see a heavy dragonfly emergence in late May to early June, and the bass certainly don't ignore it. We generally start odonate season by dropping unweighted nymph patterns below our poppers, and many days these nymphs will outfish the popper handily. We recommend dropping the nymph twelve to sixteen inches below the popper on eight-pound fluorocarbon tippet.

As far as adults go, dragonflies are not as easy for the bass to get at once hatched as damsels, but they are eaten with gusto if they find themselves struggling in the film after some ill-fated event. Dragonflies are a great choice for laid-up midafternoon fish. Fish slowly and pay attention to current breaks, and you will see them: big, lazy fish holding in choice lies watching the world go by. Throw a popper or big streamer their way and they will quickly vaporize, but present a dead-drifted dragonfly pattern on a long leader and you can watch them backpedal with it like a big western cutthroat.

Damselflies are a tremendously important insect for the smallmouth angler. They are similar to dragonflies except that they are smaller and much more numerous. Damsels emerge throughout the summer, and their numbers provide tremendous biomass for the bass. Because of this prevalence, smallmouth really respond positively to them—whether they are on the water or flying through the air. One of the more exciting spectacles to observe is smallmouth bass plucking damselflies out of midair. During calm evenings damsels flying low to the water bring smaller bass arcing through the air to intercept them midflight, reminiscent of brown trout chasing caddis and Patagonian rainbows spearing dragonflies out of midair.

That said, don't think that damsel fishing is always an aggressive, splashy game. Yes, smallmouth bass will attack these flies recklessly much of the time, but the most efficient way to fish damsels is to seek them out where they congregate en masse. The bass will be there too, sitting and salivating, waiting for one sorry bug to drift out into the danger zone. Remember that just because you don't see bass aggressively attacking living damsels doesn't mean that they aren't feeding on them. They still might be oriented to spent damsels floating flush in the film. These spent damsels congregate on weed lines and along slow, grassy, undercut banks and back eddies, and the fish that key in on them are more likely to exhibit more selective behavior. If a blue wiggly or Boogle Bug doesn't do the trick, it might be time for more imitative patterns. Find fish feeding on spent damsels and you may be fast into some of the most satisfying eats of the year.

Damselflies (above) and dragonflies (below), while both common summer foodstuffs, differ in size and profile. ERIC CHRISTENSEN/NATE SIPPLE

Flying Ants

Many watersheds across the country may experience a flying ant emergence sometime in late summer. It's at this time that ant colonies release their virgin queens and fertile male ants. What makes this emergence unique is that all colonies across a given area explode on the same day. This simultaneity increases the chances that queens and males from different colonies have an opportunity to meet, and thus increase the genetic health and complexity of the colonies. As a result, unlike the other insect emergences discussed in this book, hitting a flying ant emergence right is more often a matter of luck and chance than planning and foresight.

While it can be a difficult hatch to hit, you don't want to be caught without a handful of ant patterns, small black wigglies, and small black poppers in case you are lucky enough to find yourself in the thick of things. All the bass in the system, including the very largest fish, go on a feeding frenzy, and some fish may become selective, especially on low, ultraclear water systems. If you get an eat, be ready. It's not just small fish that eat ants. It's true that all fish, even the biggest fish in a given system, just seem to love the taste of ants, so run the heaviest tippet circumstances allow.

Not everyone is lucky enough to encounter a flying ant emergence, but those who do will definitely never forget it. NATE SIPPLE

CHAPTER 4

The Middle Column

In the "Surface" chapter we divided our fly families according to their silhouette and sonic profile on the surface. In this chapter we'll categorize flies according to how they move through the middle portion of the water column. There are three basic subcategories to middle-column flies: divers, suspending baitfish, and weighted flies. But before we begin our discussion of the flies and their presentations, let's take a closer look at the middle water column as a place to engage with the smallmouth bass.

While the middle part of the water column covers a lot of different territory and is one of the most effective places to fish for smallmouth, it wasn't always viewed as prime hunting ground for the angler. Not too long ago smallmouth

Middle-column patterns start working early in the season and remain productive through the fall. Get smart about how and where you fish them, and you'll put more fish in the net this season.

MICHAEL LESCHISIN

theorists argued that smallmouth were best targeted on the surface and on the bottom—and that those who targeted them in the middle of the water column were misled souls who might occasionally catch fish, but never as many or as large as they would above and below. Given the flies and lines available at the time, this was perhaps understandable. Poppers existed, as did dredging flies imitating large nymphs and hellgrammites, but the lessons of saltwater fly fishing hadn't yet reached the bass world, and Kelly Galloup's *Modern Streamers for Trophy Trout*, with its brave new world of fishing neutrally buoyant flies on aggressive sink tips, had yet to be written. For the modern smallmouth angler, the best point of entry into the possibilities of middle column presentation come courtesy of the Dahlberg Diver and its descendants.

When it comes to one of the richest areas of native smallmouth bass, the early reaches of the Mississippi River and its Minnesota and Wisconsin tributaries, there are two ways of looking at smallmouth fishing: before the Dahlberg Diver and after. A look at fishing trends and successes on the St. Croix River in northeastern Wisconsin, where Dahlberg developed and honed his eponymously named diver, demonstrates just how the engagement of the middle column changed the game for smallmouth anglers. To illustrate this, we'll tell the story of a prominent St. Croix River smallmouth fishing club. It

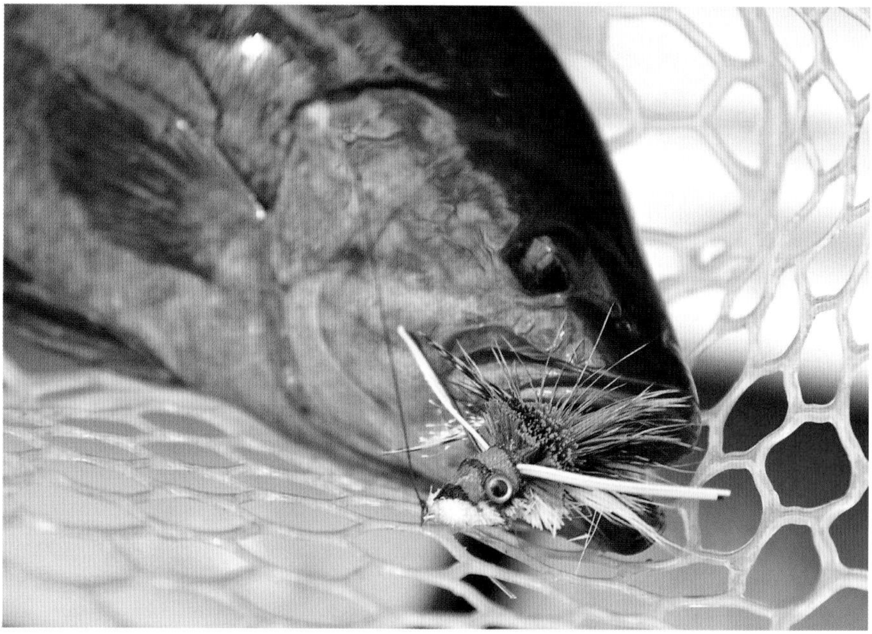

Presentation dynamics change once we head to the other side of the meniscus. Whereas previously flies were simply sound and silhouette, now they have a profile to boot. The diver represents a transitional fly that can be fished within millimeters of the surface or deeper down, depending on how it's rigged. NATE SIPPLE

was a tradition of the club to put a plaque on the wall for every bass longer than twenty inches caught on the system. For decades the number remained a low one—one or two new plaques went up on the wall every year. After the arrival of the Dahlberg Diver, however, the number changed dramatically. Now, ten to twelve gleaming plaques went up on the wall annually. It was the dawn of a new day in smallmouth fishing. The fisheries hadn't changed, of course, but the fishing sure had.

Simply put, the arrival of various middle-column flies like the diver changed the smallmouth angler's ability to engage larger fish on a consistent basis. To understand why, we'll have to look a bit closer at the different ways bass respond to silhouettes and profiles.

The Diver Family of Flies

In the words of longtime shop guide Nate Sipple, "If I personally had to fish one type of smallmouth fly for the rest of my life, it would be some kind of diver." That's high praise for the diver family of flies. But what makes a diver a diver? While writing this book we deliberated over whether to include divers in the surface chapter, since a diver will sit on the surface between strips when fished on a floating line, and can even be dead-drifted in the film if its angler were so inclined. But we ultimately concluded that the diver would be best discussed in its current spot, as a segue between true topwaters and true middle-column flies. To understand why this might be the case, let's look at the diver family of flies and identify what makes them different from the flies on either side of them in the water column.

First, there's diver anatomy. With their tapered nose and flared collar, divers are designed to dig right down into the water. In the same way that lipped minnow baits in conventional fishing achieve depth by the size and angle of their lips, divers work according to the size and angle of their heads and collars. On being fished, a diver's tapered head cuts into the water while the collar pushes the water up and the fly itself down. But divers don't all dive and swim the same way. Considerable thought, design, and variation have gone into the diver heads, as well as the materials used to producc them. Different fly designers have approached the basic design of the diver head differently. Smallmouth fly–innovator Dave Whitlock, for instance, changed angles and head design to bring us unique swimming variations of the diver like his swimming frog and swimming baitfish. Michigan guide and fly-designer Mike Schultz experiments with various foam-head designs to get his articulated divers wobbling either tightly or widely.

Top to bottom, left to right: Dahlberg Strip Diver/Larry Dahlberg, Dahlberg Diving Frog/Larry Dahlberg, Whitlock's Swimming Baitfish/Dave Whitlock, Dahlberg Diving Bug/Larry Dahlberg, Swingin' D/Mike Schultz, Bubblicious Frog/Charlie Bisharat. DAVE KARCZYNSKI

Aside from its shape, the next salient feature of the diver is the buoyancy of the head, whether made of spun deer hair or preformed foam. It's this buoyancy that brings the fly slowly back to the surface after each strip, much like the great balsa minnow patterns of the conventional fishing world. This slow-rise feature makes the diver unique among flies. Many other flies sink, but no other type of fly rises slowly to the surface on the pause. If you've ever watched a wounded minnow struggling in the film, you'll have noticed that its death spasms tend to take it below surface before it rises back gaspingly to the film—just like a diver. In sum, the diver's ability to both dive *and* rise makes it an attractive morsel to bass, but it also makes it an attractive tool for the angler, since it can be cast beyond obstructions, fished up to them, and then floated over—think logs and boulders submerged just below the surface. Where other flies would hang up, the diver can be swum over.

The last part of diver anatomy we'll discuss is the "active" part of the fly—the tail, with its array of feathers, flash, and even fur. Flash is a particularly important part of this fly—in fact, one of the ways Larry Dahlberg described the fly in its early stages was as an "underwater delivery system for Flashabou." During the active portion of the retrieve, the tail kicks out with each strip, setting the flash material into fluid undulation. But this tailing material can also entice fish during the resting part of the retrieve as a result of the interplay between materials and current. If you're wondering whether this makes the diver a suitable swing fly, you're correct. Recall that in the previous chapter we recommended divers for those new anglers who want to fish a topwater fly but have trouble with the line management required to achieve a dead drift. Whereas not many bass will eat a topwater that drags, a diver, with its tempting profile and undulating materials, fishes well no matter what you're doing to it.

The "D" in Mike Schultz's Swingin' D stands for Dahlberg. This unique homage of a pattern brings together the utility of the diver with the action of an articulated trout streamer. Fish the Swingin' D in articulated- or single-hook versions, or use lead wraps and an undersized foam head to fish deeper early or late in the season. DAVE KARCZYNSKI

As far as tailing materials go, there are three basic options: marabou, rabbit strip, and either saddle or schlappen feathers. While they all perform the same basic function, they differ in the amount of water they displace on the retrieve (with rabbit strips being the meatiest) as well as castability (with again, rabbit being heaviest). Aside from castability, you might take current speed into consideration when selecting tailing material for a diver. If you're fishing slower water, the rabbit strip is your friend: It doesn't take much to get that rippling action going. But throw a diver with a long rabbit strip tail section into faster water and it''ll get knocked around unnaturally, balling up and compressing and making that fly seem even smaller than it is. In those cases you need something with backbone, something with a stiff stem like a saddle feather that maintains its profile even in heavy flows. Schlappen would fall somewhere in between.

As we've been discussing, the smallmouth is a sound-oriented fish, and the diver certainly gives them a unique sonic profile to respond to. In distinguishing the commotion caused by a diver from that caused by a popper, think of it this way—a popper *explodes* and a diver *implodes.* That's one of the big differences between divers and larger topwater flies. Divers offer not only a different tone on the water—a percussive bass can really feel along their lateral line—but also a different direction for that tone, since the sound is pushed not only outward but down through the water column. The outsized underwater sound an imploding diver creates means that it isn't a flats- or a skinny-water fly. No: In skinny and small water, a diver is more likely to spook a fish than spur it. As such, the diver is first and foremost a structure fly, one best fished over medium to deeper water. If fish lurk down below, the diver often calls them up.

The other big difference a diver has over a conventional topwater fly is profile. Remember that by and large topwater flies possess only a silhouette. It's more or less a flat, two-dimensional shape that bass are responding to. The diver, on the other hand, adds a third dimension in the form of profile. A diver breaks the barrier of the film to present itself in full to the bass. It's that fact alone that also makes a diver a fantastic choice when the water surface is full of noise, whether in the form of chop, leaves, wind, foam, or rain. Not only do divers create a unique sound profile that will attract the fish, they also give the fish a view of itself as it separates from the top of the water column. In trout fishing, we call emergers those flies that are largely entering into our own field of vision. But this is quite anthropocentric thinking. A diver fished on a broken-water day emerges more clearly into the smallmouth's field of vision each time it's stripped, even as it moves away from our own point of view.

All things considered, divers combine some of the best features of the topwater flies we discussed (in that you can fish them slowly) with the best features of middle-column flies (they represent substantial meals).

Why, When, and Where to Fish Divers

In deciding when, where, and why to fish divers, we'll look at seasons of the year, weather events, structure fish are relating to, and even time of day.

If we're talking about times of year, the two seasons that call for regular use of divers are spring and fall—the two times of year that see significant frog migrations. It's not hard to identify when these migrations occur. In the spring, it's when you first start hearing spring peepers up and down the river corridor in the evening. In the fall, it's when you start seeing frogs everywhere at night—including pancaked on your local roads. Smallmouth know that frogs represent easy pickin's and good protein, and they will key in on these amphibians at these two times of year. These migration periods are prime time to fish divers, especially off of grassy banks.

We can also look to the weather to help us determine whether or not to fish a diver. The diver becomes an important tool in the angler's tool chest on days when smallmouth are looking up but where weather events create significant noise on the surface of the water—think rain showers and choppy

It's no coincidence that the spring and fall frog migrations coincide with a very strong diver bite.

ERIC CHRISTENSEN

water due to high winds. On such days, when the efficacy of subtle topwaters like poppers and wigglies are diminished due to lack of subsurface profile, divers can be the hot ticket.

Structure also plays a determining factor in the utility of a diver. In terms of plying the x- or y-axis, the diver is ambidexterous, particularly if fished on a floating line. Float and twitch it along the y-axis or strip it back to the boat along the x-axis. Or do both on the very same cast. Such is the versatility of the diver.

Yet another occasion to fish a diver is simply when the mood of the fish demands it. If, for some reason, you are getting looks at your poppers and wigglies but no commitments, you might need to do something to entice the fish. With the exception of the slider, one of the disadvantages of topwater fishing is the inability to make the fly look like it is "getting away." It's simply not possible to get a topwater fly up to speed that way, at least not without making it seem unnatural. But that is definitely possible with the diver. A curious fish can come up to it, and then you can make it dart away, all while presenting the fish with a much larger meal than a slider. In this way, divers can be effective tools for appealing to the chase instincts of neutral fish and getting them to commit.

Frogs become more active during evening hours. Fishing a diver at dusk on a warm spring night can induce aggressive strikes from hungry smallmouth. KYLE ZEMPEL

Similarly, divers also make a great change-of-pace fly for those hours in the middle part of the day when bass are sometimes in a stupor. If both topwater flies and middle-column baits aren't working, the diver often produces. We theorize that the diver appeals to fish that don't necessarily want to give chase (which would exclude throwing a swimming baitfish) but also want something substantial (which excludes topwater flies). For fish in that particular mood, a piece of meat dangling right in front of their nose might be too much to ignore.

Last but not least, a diver can be a great fly to fish in close over submerged wood. There are definitely times when fish are holding tight to cover and you really need to get in close to get a bass to bite. A diver fished with a short sink tip can be fished down to the wood, then paused and allowed to float up and slip over the obstruction.

HOW TO RIG AND FISH DIVERS

Divers are unique for their versatility. Fished on a floating line, we could technically almost categorize them in the surface chapter of the book. But you can also fish divers effectively without ever having them come to the surface. In a lake or very slow stretch of river, you could technically even fish the fly right on the riverbed, rising and falling off the bottom, though we wouldn't recommend this since the excess slack produced by a dragging sink tip would make this a very inefficient way to fish.

That all said, let's begin by looking at the most common way to rig a diver—with a floating line and tapered leader. In this case, it's important to note that the same leader you use for your topwater flies is definitely not going to cut it when it comes to divers: Your fly will simply not turn over. To convert a conventional nine-foot tapered leader you might use for poppers and wigglies to a diver leader, you'll need to cut the leader back to five feet or so and then add a twelve-inch section of twelve-pound test. To throw divers, beginning and certain intermediate casters may find themselves benefitting from a more aggressively weight-forward head. Shooting lines just make sense with a diver, especially since mending is generally not part of the diver game—the profile and natural fibers of the diver make it fish well on the swing.

Once we start to think about different ways of fishing subsurface in the form of sink tips (either T-11 or T-14), the diver rigging game starts to get interesting. Here's the general rule: The length of the sink tip will determine the depth the fly dives to, whereas the length of the leader will determine how high it rises afterward.

Let's say, for instance, that you are fishing in five feet of water. If you attach a five-foot section of T-14 to your floating line, you might achieve a maximum depth of three to four feet with a diver—though this will depend on the speed of the current. Now depending on the length of your leader—and length of

With their heads of spun deer hair (or foam) and ample tailing material, divers are among the most difficult flies to cast. While a shorter leader helps, there's no substitute for a tight, controlled loop and high line speed. When fishing big divers, double hauls are the norm. MICHAEL LESCHISIN

your pause between strips—that diver will rise. With a long pause, and five feet of leader, you might very well get that fly to float all they way up to the surface between strips. But cut that leader length back to, say, two feet, and vertical movement of the fly will be more constrained.

As for the retrieve itself, the two important parts of fishing a diver are sound and pause. A direct line connection with minimum slack and bowing of the line prior to the strip will help the fly break the meniscus crisply and with purpose. As was the case with poppers, the deeper the water, the more aggressive the strip (and resulting sonic implosion). In either case, incorporating long pauses that allow the fly to rise upward through the column is essential. Remember that, due to the rise, a "pause" when fishing a diver is not really a pause, at least until the fly has settled back on the surface. So even though you may feel that you are not working the fly too actively, it is in fact doing quite a bit of moving across and through the water column.

Suspending Baitfish Patterns

Each of the three subcategories of middle-column flies do something different on the pause. Divers rise. Weighted flies (which we'll get to in the third section of this chapter) drop at a speed predetermined by your weighting and mending. And neutrally buoyant minnows hang enticingly right in front of a fish's nose.

Discovering neutrally buoyant baitfish imitations in the first years of our smallmouth program is one thing that drove our early success on the rivers of northern Wisconsin. But this discovery did not come easily or painlessly; there was, as we've been noting, a fair amount of inherited trout-centric thinking to overcome. The truth of the matter is our early smallmouth fishing very much resembled trout fishing—it was, after all, how all of us learned to fly fish. Prior to the discovery of larger baitfish patterns, we fished a good deal of bugger-style flies, and the Tequeely was about as large of an offering as we ever made to a bass. Then one day Bart was out fishing behind a grandfather-grandson team in an old johnboat. With their spinning rods they spent the afternoon throwing Rapalas, and Bart couldn't believe—or accept—the degree to which they were outfishing him and his beadhead buggers. Rather than ferment in jealousy, Bart started thinking about how to duplicate their success. The next day he went through all the flies in the shop looking for something about the size of a jointed Rapala. He found it in the form of the Murdich Minnow, which the shop stocked exclusively for folks heading out East to chase stripers. He grabbed the shop's remaining supply—a scant four or five flies—and headed out the next day, curious to see what would happen when this saltwater fly hit the water. As far as we know Bart was, on that fateful morning, the first guy to ever throw a saltwater baitfish pattern on the warm-water rivers of northern Wisconsin. When Bart reared back and delivered that Murdich, it was the largest fly he had ever thrown at a smallmouth bass.

The fish went nuts.

That evening Bart got on the phone with the Umpqua rep to order some Murdiches for the shop, only to find out that they were being discontinued due to poor sales. They did, however, have some unsold inventory collecting dust in a back room.

"How many?" Bart asked.

"A hundred and fifty dozen," came the Umpqua rep's reply.

Bart didn't miss a beat with his answer: "Send them all."

Since those early days the varieties of mid-column baitfish patterns have proliferated greatly, and we now live in a time of unprecedented streamer abundance and innovation. But, while today's mid-column baitfish pattern

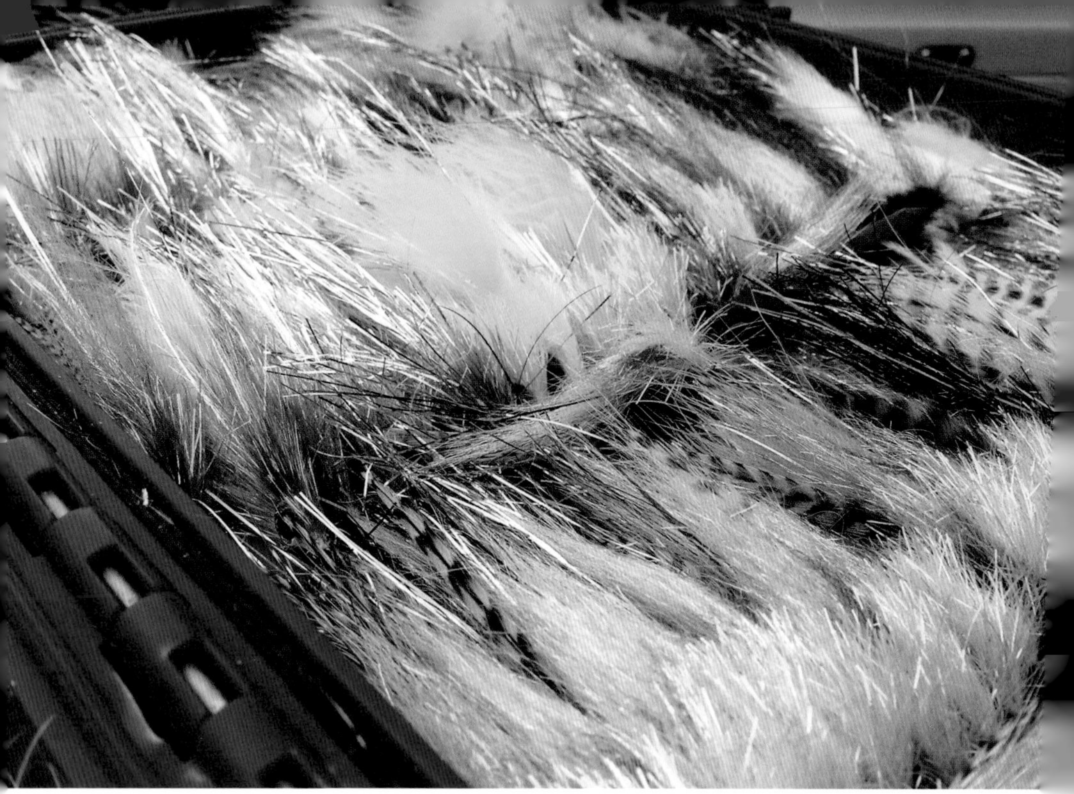

This box of neutrally buoyant baitfish patterns is ready for action. In general, you can expect flashy, synthetic flies to fish better as time wears on. A brand-new synthetic fly can be difficult to get below the meniscus with a floating line. But as it accrues grime and oils from contact with fish, it will become easier to manipulate and fish. NATE SIPPLE

comes in many sizes, styles, and materials, there's one thing they all have in common. Fished correctly they scream loudly, right in a bass's face: "Eat me! Clearly there's something not quite right about me. I'm either wounded or disoriented or both. Whatever the case, please put me out of my misery." That telegraphing of vulnerability is an essential part of the mid-column baitfish presentation equation. Simply put, bass (along with all predatory fish) have evolved to respond directly to distress signals put out by fish.

An experiment we conducted in the shop a few years ago demonstrates just how fine-tuned smallmouth bass are to injured baitfish. For a few weeks of the summer, we kept a juvenile smallmouth in a large fish tank in the shop in order to study how it ate various foodstuffs. One of the most telling things we learned was how that bass reacted to a scoop of minnows dropped into the tank. The moment the cluster bomb of minnows hit the water, the bass would erupt—but he wouldn't eat indiscriminately. Quite the opposite, in fact. During the first few minutes after the minnows were delivered, our aquarium bass would pick off every single weak or crippled minnow. The hunting of healthier minnows would take place later, and only after there was nothing weak left to eat. On

average it would take three to four days before he finally ate the strongest, healthiest fish. The takeaway, in case it isn't obvious, is this: You want your baitfish patterns to swim like there's something wrong with them.

When, Where, and Why to Fish Suspending Baitfish Patterns

Neutrally buoyant baitfish patterns are the most versatile tools in the angler's arsenal for a number of reasons. First off, they can be fished quickly, slowly, or somewhere in between—and you can do all three inside of a single cast. This makes them unique among the other fly families in this book. Topwater flies cannot be fished as quickly, and weighted and dredging patterns cannot be fished as slowly, at least not without the risk of hanging up.

Neutrally buoyant baitfish patterns can also cover a lot of water. This makes them a great pattern to use when hunting new water, or returning to water that looks a good deal different from the last time you fished it (whether higher after a rain event or lower after a drought). The fact that they can be cast a distance with minimal disturbance on splashdown means that they are a good subsurface alternative to topwaters when it comes to fishing large shallow or mid-depth flats. In fact, on especially large flats where fish are spread out, we'll often turn to baitfish patterns before topwater flies, since they allow us to cover considerably more water. Mid-column baitfish are definitely our number-one flats fly in the early season where fish are feeding on shallow flats but have not yet keyed into surface bugs. We tend to throw slightly smaller patterns at this time. Larger versions are great later in the season when fish are congregated in transition areas and are looking to put on weight quickly. Musky anglers know all too well how regularly smallmouth eat their oversized fall musky patterns—which are by and large simply much larger neutrally buoyant baitfish patterns.

For moderate to weak casters, the enticing action of baitfish patterns means fish can be called in from a distance. And so anglers who might not be able to hit their casting targets with consistency might consider throwing baitfish to increase their chances of moving a fish. The same cannot necessarily be said for topwater flies and crayfish patterns.

Lastly, because neutrally buoyant baitfish patterns tend to be among the easiest flies to cast and manipulate, they are also good for dealing with fish in a variety of moods. For one, they can be cast a distance and on a long leader if necessary, making flies in this family a reasonable choice for wary fish in low, clear water. Another advantage is that they can be retrieved in a variety of ways. It can be difficult to customize a wiggly or crayfish presentation for an ornery

In the hands of an experienced caster, neutrally buoyant baitfish patterns can cover a lot of water. In this image, a long cast will allow the angler to work the first shelf and second shelf as well as midstream weed beds or rock gardens. The most efficient baitfish anglers will use their eyes to identify the most productive possible retrieve route along the x-axis. Not all are created equal.

MICHAEL LESCHISIN

bass that is following the fly but not committing. But baitfish imitations can be made to swim in a variety of ways depending on how they are stripped. Lastly, because you can cast them far, land them quietly, and strip them quickly, baitfish patterns also allow you to hit multiple spots within a single cast. Make a cast parallel to a sweeper, fish that spot deliberately, then throw in some slack or strip it in quickly to entice something out of that midstream rock.

All of this makes neutrally buoyant baitfish patterns a great prospecting and diagnostic tool. On any given day you'll know where the fish are, what mood they are in, and what it will take on your part to translate their curiosity into gluttony.

How a Bass Eats a Baitfish

How a bass eats a baitfish helps us to make the right decisions about where to place the hook in a given pattern. And it's a pretty easy decision. Basically, you don't need to worry about where your hook is located—as long as it's in the front. Smallmouth are efficient eaters of baitfish. If a smallmouth wants to eat a minnow, it eats it headfirst, regardless of the size of the bass or your fly. Even in the case of a six-inch smallmouth eating a six-inch Murdich, the bass will still be eating the fly headfirst, with just a few bucktail tips and a bit of flash sticking out beyond its jaw.

We sometimes observe anglers who blame the fly for missed fish. "He short-struck it and didn't get the hook," these anglers will erroneously claim after

It's no wonder that bass associate flash with food. ERIC CHRISTENSEN

failing to stick a bass, even we were able to see that the fly had completely disappeared into the fish's mouth between strips. "Should have had a stinger hook," they will continue. We only shake our heads. A collective five thousand river trips from everyone who's contributed to this book will tell you that when it comes to baitfish patterns, you never need to worry about where your hook is located—as long (one more time) as it's in the front. This fact lies in stark contrast to trout, where articulated flies are necessary to ensure consistent quality hookups. The takeaway? When tying baitfish patterns for *Micropterus dolomieu*, one hook will do.

Types of Suspending Baitfish Patterns

The essence of the mid-column baitfish imitation, be it a Murdich Minnow, Barto Minnow, Flash Monkey, or Gartside Soft Hackle, is that between strips they hang there, neutrally buoyant, in front of the fish's face, daring a following bass to eat, or a distant bass to swim over and engage. And indeed, it's this neutrally buoyant hang that often gets curious fish to commit to eating. We've seen countless fish follow a Murdich for twenty to thirty feet, only to inhale it during one of the long pauses where the fly hung right on the fish's nose. In fact, it's due to the appetizing nature of the hang that so many jerkbaits and soft plastics in the gear-fishing world also possess this feature. The one advantage that flies have over lures, however, is that they can move even when they're not moving. Whether it's the Flashabou, marabou, or some other material, one thing all good baitfish patterns have in common is some sort of ability to breathe when paused. This breathing is the trigger that most smallmouth can't resist!

Another thing that all baitfish patterns possess is some level of flash. There is good reason for this. Earlier in this section we discussed how finely attuned smallmouth are to wounded things. And indeed one of the main signals of vulnerability in a real-life injured baitfish is flash. Regular, pronounced flash is not all that common in the watery world. It occurs when a baitfish's body tilts awkwardly, which tends to happen only when a small fish is under duress. So how can fly anglers best capitalize on a smallmouth's susceptibility to injured fish? By incorporating some degree of flash into every mid-column baitfish pattern you tie, or insisting on flash in every baitfish pattern you buy.

So we've established that all the baitfish patterns discussed in this section hang when the retrieve is paused and offer some element of flash to appeal to the bass's lust for distress. So how are they different? There are three fundamentally important ways we distinguish neutrally buoyant baitfish patterns

Left to right, top to bottom: Drunk & Disorderly/Tom Lynch, Swingin' D/Mike Schultz, CK Baitfish/Chuck Kraft, Brush Hog/Russ Maddin, Chicken Changer/Mike Schultz, Hot Flash Minnow/Andy Burk, Flash Monkey/Russ Maddin, Murdich Minnow/Bill Murdich, Gartside Soft Hackle/Jack Gartside, Barto Minnow/Bart Landwehr, Mirage Minnow/Charlie Piette, Midnight Mullet/Michael Conner. DAVE KARCZYNSKI

from each other: the commotion they make upon landing, the amount of water they displace when stripped, and the intensity of their action.

All other things being equal, the quietest landings are accomplished with a floating line; its taper allows excellent loop and line speed control. Weighted lines—even intermediate lines—are going to land a bit harder. This is important to note because some neutrally buoyant baitfish patterns require intermediate lines (or even more aggressive sinking lines) to swim correctly, even if just below the surface. Two terrific suspending baitfish patterns from Michigan are Russ Maddin's Flash Monkey and Mike Schultz's Swingin' D. The fact that both have a large profile, push plenty of water, and exude ostentatious action makes them great big-water search patterns. But put either on a floating line and it's just going to skate awkwardly at the surface. These and other big, especially buoyant flies need to be thrown on sinking lines, which, due to their being aerodynamic, generate more speed than floating lines, resulting in slightly more commotion on splashdown. Moderate to big splashdowns definitely have their place, however, for instance when fishing stained water, when fishing big water, and when pursuing a reaction strike—that is,

Not all baitfish patterns are synthetic and full of flash. These Deceivers are composed entirely of bucktail and saddle feathers. They might not cast quite as easily as a synthetic fly, but the natural materials will certainly pulse more in the water. Lefty Kreh liked to throw this pattern into deep, gyring eddies with a full sinking line and let it descend through the column with hardly a twitch—the swirling current would see to it that motion was imparted. More often than not, the result was a good-size bass. ERIC CHRISTENSEN

when fishing large flies very loudly and aggressively over the course of many river miles, looking for those few angry fish that are just looking for something to take their anger out on.

The quietest landing, on the other hand, would come from largely or entirely synthetic baitfish patterns thrown on a floating line. That's because synthetic materials absorb little or no water and therefore don't accrue extra weight while they are being fished. A Murdich Minnow—especially a smaller one—lands almost as softly as a topwater fly, and it is an excellent choice for fishing extremely shallow water to spooky, flats-hunting fish.

One tip for fishing suspending baitfish patterns with a high proportion of synthetic materials: Get it used and keep it wet. Fresh-out-of-the-box synthetic flies are naturally hydrophobic and have trouble sinking, and even an older fly will sit on the surface of the water if you false cast all the water out of it. All of these neutrally buoyant flies fish much better after becoming waterlogged, and they fish even better after getting slimed with a few fish. If you want to expedite the sinking and sliming process, you can use a sink expedient such as Henry's Sinket by Loon Outdoors.

The amount of water a fly pushes is also important. Flies with big heads, especially flies with foam, possum, wool heads, or laser dub heads, move a lot of water on the strip, making them good choices when water is stained, flows are heavy, and fish are relying on their lateral lines to hunt. As noted above, flies with big heads tend to require a sinking line or sink tip to get below the surface of the water, since that large head also creates a footprint that makes it hard for the fly to break through the meniscus. Because these larger heads carry more water and create more sound on splashdown, they might not be the best choice on a skinny flat.

On the opposite end of the water displacement spectrum we have flies like Jack Gartside's Soft Hackle Streamer. The head on this fly tapers to a very fine point. This is a fly to fish in clear water, especially low, clear water, when fish are feeding primarily by sight. At such times a large, aggressive, wake-pushing fly might be overkill.

The Murdich Minnow, on the other hand, is an example of an in-between fly in terms of water displacement and action. Its medium-size head appeals to a fish's lateral line while not overwhelming it. Fish it more slowly in shallow clear water or quickly and more aggressively in stained water to get the fish's attention. The versatility and adaptability of the Murdich is part of what makes it one of the great smallmouth bass flies of all time.

Articulated patterns from the trout world have a time and place in bass fishing. This Drunk & Disorderly moves with a wild, erratic action that can sometimes serve as a skeleton key for particularly acute cases of lockjaw. Note the extra buoyant deer-hair head. This fly will require a sinking line to keep it swimming correctly. NATE SIPPLE

The sinuous movement of Blane Chocklett's Feathered Game Changer comes from a combination of natural materials and several short, connected shanks. It's a deadly fly fished slowly and on the swing, which means it catches fish just as readily in the spring and fall as it does in the summer.
NATE SIPPLE

When it comes to action, quiet flies—those flies with a subtle wiggle or pulsing action—are generally best for lower, clearer water and warier fish. The Soft Hackle Streamer, like many tied-in-the-round marabou streamers, has more of a pulsing, jellyfish action than a side-to-side action, and this subtler action again makes it attractive to fish in low, clear water. Conversely, a baitfish pattern bashing about like it's on PCP on a shallow, calm flat will sometimes put off more fish than it turns on. Flies with exaggerated side-to-side movements are better when casting over deeper water and structure. These flies are also easier to see at a distance (for both the angler and the bass).

Putting It All Together

Got fish cruising on a shallow flat? Looking to cast to fish hunting on the first shelf? Time for a floating line and a Murdich Minnow or Gartside Soft Hackle. Conversely, if you're throwing flies in heavier, deeper water above the second shelf or on the edges of deep holes and logjams, especially after a rain event, throw on a sink tip culminating with a Flash Monkey, Swingin' D, or Feather Game Changer.

Rigging Suspending Patterns

Line choice when it comes to fishing neutrally buoyant baitfish patterns is often a matter of flexibility. Given that most (but not all) of these patterns can be fished on a floating line, we favor the same lines we use for topwater presentations—the advantage being that you can switch back and forth between topwater and baitfish presentations without too much fuss. By adding a length of sink tip or poly tip you can also fish most ultrabouyant patterns effectively. If you fish large, ultrabouyant baitfish patterns regularly, you might consider keeping two baitfish rods at the ready, one with a floating line (for topwaters and light baitfish patterns) and a short-tip sinking line for bigger, more aggressive offerings.

Fishing Suspending Baitfish Patterns

Neutrally buoyant baitfish patterns probably have the most far-ranging applications throughout the smallmouth seasons. They work before the topwater strike begins in the spring and extend after it finishes in the fall. You can fish them on a floating line just subsurface or even on a sinking line down and deep. Neutrally buoyant batifish patterns are, in short, a true mainstay of smallmouth angling. Learn how to use these flies and you will have a fish-catching tool that serves you well throughout the year.

That said, fishing these patterns in the most effective way possible requires a bit of inverted thinking. We anglers, and especially anglers who also fish for trout, tend to think of the strip as the primary action in the retrieve. After all, it's the strip that gives a fly life, right? That may be true, but if the strip is the thing that garner's curiosity, it's the pause that most often entices a bass to bite. Thus, in trying to think of how to approach fishing baitfish patterns, try thinking of the pause as the main event and the strip as the in-between motion that gets you from one main event to the other. We tell our clients that we don't care if they twitch/strip the minnow one time or six times, it's the "pause and hang" that will trigger the eat. This is one of the things that makes the smallmouth bass unique from other predator fish. In musky fishing, a change of direction is often needed to convert a following fish into an eating fish. Brown trout responding to a skating, racing streamer will stop on a dime and refuse if the fly stops moving. In the saltwater game, the fly is rarely or never stopped. But a smallmouth likes to eat its food when it's paused and swooning right in front of its nose.

While mid-column baitfish imitations are at their most enticing when hanging there mid-column between strips, it's still important not to get too rhythmic with those strips. We've seen hundreds of times when the two anglers in the boat are throwing the exact same baitfish imitation. In this situation the guy in front should be cleaning up, since he's getting first cast at everything. Instead, it's the guy in back who's outfishing him five to one. What gives? Our experience tells us that when this happens the guy in the front has probably turned into a human metronome. A methodical retrieve with regular-size strips and regular-length pauses is just no good when it comes to smallmouth fishing. One of the more fascinating things about streamer fishing is how the attitude of the angler gets telegraphed into the stripped fly. An angler lulled into a daydreaming stupor will transmit that same sense of stupor over to the fly. A fish looks at a fly pulled by a checked-out angler and there's just not enough erraticism to signal distress. Our experimentations have told us time and again that distress is what fish are looking for, and distress results from excited, unpredictable actions. For this reason, it can be a good idea to occasionally use the rod to manipulate the fly in addition to the strip. It just keeps things from getting boring for the angler. Our best baitfish anglers have strong casting forearms for using the rod to throw sharp, calculated actions into a stripped fly. In short, when fishing neutrally buoyant baitfish patterns, throw some diversity into your retrieves. By all means don't fish like a robot!

The angle of the fly to the fish is also important. Suspending baitfish patterns fish best when they can be presented broadside to the fish. They lose much of their appeal when cast directly upstream and fished down. In such cases, the flies discussed at the end of this chapter—the Tequeelys, Circus Peanuts, and Clousers—are better options, since they can derive their action from a subtle jigging motion. It's also worth noting that the Murdich, Flash Monkey, and other side-to-side patterns achieve their enticing action during what we'll refer to as the "recovery" part of the strip. Your strip pulls the fly forward, but when that forward pull ceases, the friction of the head in the water forces the fly to turn—but the fly can't turn, or can't turn much, if the line is taut. The necessity of a soft (not taut) connection after each strip means we must pay attention to boat control. In addition to the angler practicing good line hygiene, the oarsmen should be moving the boat at roughly the same speed as the current to prevent drag on the line when there shouldn't be any.

While talking about topwater flies in the previous chapter, we emphasized the importance of letting the fly marinate or stew after landing—in fishing baitfish patterns, we advocate for the exact opposite. That is, you should begin your retrieve the moment your fly hits the water. There are two reasons for this. First off, sitting on or in the film, baitfish patterns don't look like food. While topwater flies present a distinctly foody silhouette to a fish,

Lake bass love baitfish patterns, too. The crystal-clear waters of the Great Lakes shorelines make sight fishing to cruising smallmouth a successful and exciting way to fish. River anglers should take special note of the light color of lake fish and calibrate their vision accordingly when scanning the flats for likely targets. LUKE KAVAJECZ

either a frog, small mammal, or some aquatic insect, baitfish do not (try dead-drifting a "new" Murdich Minnow on the film and you'll see what we mean). These flies are all about demonstrating crippled movement and showing a full underwater profile.

The more important reason to begin your retrieve immediately is to take advantage of a fish's native reactions to something of size moving through its home space. A baitfish landed out of the sky may startle a bass, and stripping immediately gives you the best chance of converting that surprise to anger. If a fish is in the area, don't surprise him and then give him a chance to inspect. Rather, surprise him and force him to make a decision: fight or flight. The sight of a fleeing baitfish is a natural bite trigger for smallmouth, so practice a "splat and strip" with fishing baitfish patterns to jar any nearby fish into a reaction bite.

We've seen it happen hundreds of times where a smallmouth turns and looks at a baitfish pattern the instant it hits the water, only to turn and swim away if the fly isn't moved. This usually happens when an angler shoots a cast and then fumbles with the line afterwards, or has to unwrap it from the butt of the rod (it happens). The importance of giving your fly action immediately upon landing means you need to practice good "line hygiene" throughout

Good line hygiene is essential at all points of the baitfish game. Practice eliminating excess or clumsy movements with the line hand when transitioning from casting to stripping and you'll be ready for strikes that occur immediately after the fly has landed. MICHAEL LESCHISIN

your cast. This means using your line hand (usually your left hand) to make an "O" that functions as the first guide the line will pass through, before your stripping guide even. This will not only afford longer casts, but it will prevent your line from fouling around the reel or butt of the rod.

Although you want to start moving the fly immediately, that is not the same thing as fishing the fly aggressively. Especially if you are fishing y-axis structure with a finite bite window, you don't want to run the fly out of the zone immediately. Thus, the best way to fish these baits immediately after landing is to give them a few short, immediate twitches—moves that pull the fly below the surface and get them moving without pulling them out of the feeding zone. You can elongate your strips later in the retrieve, but upon landing, keep them sudden and short.

Last but not least, when it comes to fishing suspending baitfish patterns successfully, there is the length of the presentation to consider. The efficient middle-column angler does not fish through dead parts of the cast. Of course, on a flat or a piece of x-axis structure where bass can be anywhere, a fly can and should be fished all the way back to the boat. But sometimes the structural orientation suggests doing otherwise. If you are fishing y-axis structure from a moving boat—say, a second shelf—the efficient way to make presentations is to cast slightly behind the shelf, work the fly fifteen feet past the ledge, then pick up the fly and cast again. This is not to suggest that smallmouth don't follow flies long distances. They do, and if you've got a follower then by all means work the retrieve back as long as you need to. But in most circumstances we firmly believe that covering more water with short, efficient presentations is ultimately going to be a much more productive method of fishing than fishing out every cast for longer than is necessary. Efficient presentations that don't "overstay their welcome" are key to becoming a better middle-column angler.

Special Situations: Skipping under Obstructions

One way to fish shady, tree-covered overhangs, docks, and piers is to work the underneath areas with a skipped synthetic baitfish pattern. This is an especially effective midday tactic when fish are trying to avoid direct overhead sunlight. If you've watched the Bassmaster's Classic, you've seen bass anglers

Be it docks or low bridges, overhead cover provides smallmouth with a sense of safety. Getting efficient with sidearm casting angles will help you make difficult but high-percentage casts on the water without missing your target or getting hung up. DAVE KARCZYNSKI

skipping soft plastics deep beneath these shadowy overhead structures. You can duplicate this by fishing a high-density integrated sinking line (for example, a type VI), a long tapered leader (nine feet), and an unweighted synthetic fly, like a Murdich Minnow. The high-density sinking line will allow you to achieve terrifically high line speeds, the near-weightless fly will allow for very tight loops, the long leader will catapult your fly deep beneath the dock, and the natural hydrophobic quality of the synthetic materials ensures your fly will skip across, not stick to, the water's surface. Use a sidearm cast, and get your fly moving the instant it hits the water for reactionary strikes.

The Importance of Using Your Eyes

With suspending baitfish patterns, your ability to perceive following fish becomes an important part of your skill set—in fact, vision is one of those things that separates good anglers from great ones. Vision is important for a few reasons. For one, it allows anglers to know how and when to manipulate the fly. In the case of a fish following the fly, the when is just as important as the how. Too much action and speed and a following fish could become deterred and swim off. Too little and the fish could lose interest. Reading the body language of a sighted fish that's following a fly comes with years of experience and is, frankly, one of those things you need to screw up a bunch of times before you get it right.

Vision also aids immensely with bite detection. Remember that smallmouth are famous "on the pause" eaters. This presents an element of difficulty in detecting the strike since the ability to feel the hit may not be there during a longer pause between strips. And the hit can be very brief. Due to their love of crayfish, smallmouth have developed a remarkable ability to expel food from their mouths with gusto. If you've ever watched a smallmouth eating a crayfish, it basically inhales and exhales them on the same beat. While it certainly isn't mistaking a baitfish for a crayfish, once a bass recognizes that the fly is not food it will use that exhale faculty to reject your fly. Since you may have a short window in which to act, the best way to know when to set the hook is to see the eat.

Of course, the ability to track a following fish only happens with the ability to track and follow your fly. While fish see a number of different colors well underwater, the same can't be said for the human eye. Fishing white, when possible, not only gives you the ability to see your fly better, it will help with the process of developing and using your vision. Everyone can see the fly disappear, but if you can see a smallmouth pursuing the fly, then you can

One of the skills that separates guides from anglers is the ability to see following fish. Whether fishing topwaters or middle-column flies, getting a good visual read on the situation allows you to convert more follows and have better timing on hook sets. This begins with knowing what the fish in your river system look like from above. Fish in some systems will be darker, others lighter. Knowing what you're looking for will help you distinguish both resting and traveling fish from other visual elements in the river, such as small boulders and logs. NATE SIPPLE

manipulate it into eating. You can convert the follow into a bite. You can become a better angler. This is why so many of our suspending baitfish imitations are white in color.

The color of following fish, however, will vary by watershed and by region, so part of developing good vision comes with practice and knowing what to look for. Smallmouth have different coloration in different parts of the country. Do your smallmouth look darker than the surrounding water? Lighter? As a general rule, the darker the water, the darker the fish. The fish of the tea-stained rivers of Wisconsin, Minnesota, and Michigan are a stark contrast to the light-green fish of Door County, Wisconsin. The water there is gin clear and the fish, suited to their environment, are very "clean" looking with little in the way of bars, stripes, or the iconic bronze coloration.

Once you are able to see your fly and know what sort of fish coloration to expect, developing vision is all about using your peripherals. As you move the fly forward through the water, you should be aware of your fly but actively looking at an area several square feet larger than the fly moving through it. We are often looked at as ninjas by clients for our ability to see a fish on a fly long before they can. Aside from staring into the water at flies a lot more than they do, it's how we are looking at the situation that makes the difference. We tell our clients that they should be looking at a moving hula hoop of water that has the fly as its bull's-eye. That's right, imagine your fly as the center point of a big imaginary hula hoop, then focus almost more on the "around the fly" water than the fly itself. By learning to watch around the fly, you can often see fish tracking from a distance and can then make the kind of changes in retrieve necessary for commitment. Of course, sometimes we don't necessarily see the fish itself. Oftentimes we simply get a glimpse of "something different"—an unnatural surface movement, a shadow where there shouldn't be one, a strange flutter of the fly that suggests something has just grazed it. Time is the only thing that will allow you to see these subtle parts of the sport.

Setting the Hook

The strip set is not our preferred method for setting the hook with most smallmouth applications, and suspending baitfish patterns are no different (the exception being when fishing sinking lines with larger profile patterns).

Unlike brown trout, bass may attack a fly several times throughout the course of a retrieve if it does not get stuck by the hook. So if you fail to hook up on a bass, don't despair. Simply continue working your fly as before, and be ready: More often than not, you will get a second chance. KYLE ZEMPEL

The strip set many times does not get a good angle on the fish's mouth to be effective: By using a rod set, we are more likely to set the hook up and into the fish's jaw rather than pulling it straight out of a fish's mouth. In short: Eliminating any slack created in the retrieve with a strip, followed by a quick hard rod set when the fly comes tight to the fish, will help the hook achieve the kind of purchase that keeps it stuck.

Another good reason to avoid strip setting when fishing suspending baitfish patterns is because smallmouth will follow a fly and "eat through it," as we like to say, grabbing the fly, spitting it out, and grabbing it again. In the case of a missed attempt to eat, a strip set pulls the fly too far away from the fish too quickly. In the case that a fish attempts to eat and misses, a rod set will move the fly only a short distance away—you'll still have plenty of opportunity for a second strike. In short, a rod set will not take your fly out of play in case you fail to hook up, whereas a strip set usually will end your chance at that particular fish.

Sinking Flies

So far in this chapter we've talk about divers, which dive down and float up, and neutrally buoyant flies, which hang right in front of a fish's face. The last type of fly we'll deal with in this middle of the column chapter are the weighted middle-column flies. Fished on a floating line, they represent the inverse to divers in terms of their movements through the water, sinking on the pause and chasing the line upward on the retrieve. They can be fished aggressively with regular strips along the x-axis, but unlike both divers and suspended baitfish patterns, sinking flies can also achieve a true sustained mid-column y-axis presentation if desired. Sinking middle-column flies represent one of the most densely populated fly pattern families in the smallmouth catalog, with plenty of crossover patterns from the trout world.

In the grand scheme of this book, sinking flies also form a natural segue to the bottom-column flies and techniques found in the next chapter. In fact, some of these flies can be fished effectively as deep-stripping or dredging patterns. But for our current purposes, however, we're defining middle-column flies as weighted flies fished on floating lines and tapered leaders.

From an anatomical point of view, flies in this family are unique. Unlike baitfish patterns, flies in the sinking category are often tied in the round, which is to say, they present the same profile to a fish no matter what the angle of viewing. They also tend to incorporate rubber legs in a variety of interesting ways. And, of course, they possess weight, either in the form of a helmet, barbell eyes, lead wraps, a conehead, or some combination thereof.

When fished on a floating line, sinking flies such as the Clouser allow the boat or wading angler maximum range through the water column. Upstream and downstream mending as well as changes in rates of retrieve allow a fly to drop into a bucket one moment and swim over an obstruction the next. ERIC CHRISTENSEN

Within this general category of sinking flies, we'll further distinguish between "wafting flies"—flies like the Tequeely or Woolly Bugger that sink slowly and make great y-axis presentation flies—and "jig flies" like the Clouser or Circus Peanut. Of course, if you tie your own flies you can achieve different sink rates by working with different plummeting agents and materials. A wafting fly can be repurposed as a jig fly, and vice versa, but doing so sometimes negates a given pattern's fish-attracting power: A bugger made to twitch, ripple, and breathe in the current on a slow waft loses some of its magic if you jig it, just as a Circus Peanut made to aggressively shake its rubber and marabou in a fish's face loses potency when it's just floating along. That said, it's still a good idea to tie your mid-column sinking patterns in at least two sink rates. These sink rates will allow you not only to fish higher or lower in the column, but also faster or slower, depending on the mood of the fish and the conditions at hand.

Rigging Sinking Middle-Column Flies

As just mentioned, we fish sinking middle-column flies on a floating line with a tapered leader—plain and simple. The best lines for this situation tend to be presentation lines, that is, conventionally tapered weight-forward lines, since the ability to perform aerial and on-the-water mends becomes important when we want to either get a sinking fly to fall more quickly (in which case we'd perform a tuck cast) or move sinking flies along the y-axis either for part or the whole of a presentation. As far as leaders go, you can manipulate several aspects of the terminal end to micromanage sink rate, which in the case of a jigging fly also translates to increased severity of the jigging motion. Fish deeper and jig more aggressively by deploying a longer, thinner tippet section, and/or attaching your fly with a loop knot, since a loop will allow the fly to plummet in streamlined fashion, weight-first through the water column. Conversely, you can run shallower and have a subtler jigging motion with a shorter length of slightly heavier tippet material and/or a direct connection knot.

When, Where, and Why to Fish Sinking Middle-Column Flies

Sinking middle-column flies fish well throughout the year and provide a particularly important transition between the dredging flies of the early season and the upper-column presentations of true summer. In terms of structure, sinking middle-columns flies can be very effective tools for fishing bottoms with irregular structure and variable depth, since they can be lowered and raised through the water column via mends and strips. Flies in this family are also great for fishing spots on spots, especially in quick water. Unlike suspending baitfish patterns that must move immediately back toward the boat on landing to be effective, sinking middle-column flies allow you to hang them in front of the fish's face for a second or two before beginning the retrieve. This makes them a great choice for hot-spotting: Plunk these flies down behind boulders and sweepers, alongside bridge pilings, and beside sheer cliffs. Be ready for near-instant action: These flies bust through the film and start fishing immediately, whether you are ready or not.

Mid-column sinking flies are some of the best ways to pick the lock on low water fish relating to wood. On slow, clear, sandy rivers, low summer water can be an especially challenging time to fish. Without recourse to sufficiently

Left to right, top to bottom: Kreelex Minnow/Chuck Kraft, Clouser Deep Minnow/Bob Clouser, Autumn Splendor/Tim Heng, Curly Tail Critter Bug/Chuck Kraft, Mud Bug/Nelson Ham, Olive Strip ESL/Charlie Piette, Clawdad/Chuck Kraft, Circus Peanut/Russ Maddin, Conehead Madonna/Kelly Galloup, Tequeely, Gonga/Charlie Craven, Coffey's Sparkle Minnow/Greg Coffey. DAVE KARCZYNSKI

deep water, fish hold terrifically tight to timber and need to be cajoled out. Sometimes a fish will give its position up for a gently placed topwater fly, but in the lowest, clearest water even this movement away from the safety of fallen timber can be too much. Enter a small, slow-falling, lightly weighted fly. To present properly to wood, set up your cast so that you land well upstream of the wood, then mend to waft the fly over and through the wood. Try grazing the wood, and don't worry about doing too much to the fly—touch mending works wonders in this situation. By deploying this technique on difficult late summer days, the change in the success of your fishing day can be dramatic. One moment you're on a river seemingly devoid of life, the next three smallmouth materialize from a log and fight one another for your fly. And the ones you don't hook will disappear into the wood as quickly as they came.

Wafting flies can be fished very subtly, and doing so can salvage an otherwise slow day on the water when nothing seems to be working. Take that most preeminent of wafting flies, the Tequeely. Its rubber legs act as a kind of parachute, affording it a terrifically slow sink rate. When you think about it, it's actually very much a mid-column wiggly, and it can be fished with touch mends, just like a wiggly can. Challenge yourself to fish the Tequeely and other wafting flies without stripping. When presented from a moving boat, it's very possible to fish all the way down a run and never have to strip the fly one time. A series of mends is all that is required to add movement to the fly. Wafting is a fantastic technique to use when the "less is more" rule is in effect, as it often is in late summer.

Depending on how quickly or deeply you fish them, jig flies like Clousers and Circus Peanuts may be a visual or tactile game—or a little of both. They get down quick, which makes them great for fishing much deeper wood and holes. But deeper water is not the only occasion for a jig fly. Because they begin fishing immediately and by essentially hanging in place (whereas a neutrally buoyant baitfish imitation has to be stripped), weighted flies are great for casting to specific, small-window ambush lies where fish are actively looking to feed—think current seams just behind a significant obstruction. They are also great for hitting small, mid-depth pockets, such as small, single-fish lies behind shallow boulders. Fish in these positions are usually as aggressive as they come. Note that casting accuracy and aerial mending must be refined for this technique to be as advantageous as possible.

Submerged wood is a late-summer, low-water bass magnet. While typically we'd approach a lie like this with a quiet topwater fly, sometimes asking the bass to leave their safe spot and travel to the surface is requesting too much. At such times, a quiet, lightly weighted sinking fly fished just over the wood—and therefore just inches from a bass's nose—can be the right fly for the job. NATE SIPPLE

Last but not least, for the wading angler, weighted flies presented with a floating line offer a chance to present to fish directly upstream and downstream from them. In terms of upstream presentations, a lightly weighted fly presented in front of and off to the side of a fish, like you'd present a dry fly for trout, can be effective when downstream presentations aren't effective or perhaps even possible (during low water on a very small river, for instance). Fishing deeper water downstream requires a different approach. Identify the target water, present from upstream, and immediately start stack mending to gain the required depth. Then come tight and shake and strip the fly through the target water, throwing in small mends to create the pause that smallmouth respond to so aggressively.

Swinging the Middle Column

The middle column is a great and relatively easy place to swing flies, either with a single-handed or two-handed rod. Swinging the middle column gives the wading angler a chance to cover a lot of water, to fish delicately at a distance, and to make slow, in-your-face presentations in heavy flows. Unlike stripping streamers from a moving boat, swinging flies from a fixed wading position is a fundamentally slow approach. But it also shows the fly to a lot of fish.

There are plenty of circumstances in which swinging the middle column makes a lot of sense, and one of the best is small, clear, spring-creek-style water. On this type of water, presentations often need to be made at a distance, and softly, especially when the water is low. On such occasions, slow swinging an unweighted leech or baitfish pattern on a floating line can be a truly deadly way to fish. A long, quartering cast and a few stack mends will get the fly stealthily into position in front of a prime lie. When choosing middle-column swing patterns, look for unweighted or lightly weighted patterns that land lightly but are full of longer, natural fibers. Rabbit strips, marabou, and schlappen feathers all move well with current, but so do certain synthetic materials, such as craft fur. Leech patterns can be swung straight, whereas baitfish patterns benefit from a bit of pulsing. But don't overwork the fly. Smallmouth, especially big smallmouth, welcome easy meals, and when slow swinging you are relying on your fly's materials, not your hands, to seal the deal. We're sometimes surprised by how little we have to do to coax big spring-creek smallmouth out of logjams. Tie slow-swing flies with a minimum of material, and experiment with different gauge hooks for weight instead of adding lead or eyes, which often add *too* much weight. Bites will come in the form of either subtle or not-so-subtle tugs, at which point all that's usually required is a sharp raising of the

Flies with a little bit of weight and a lot of natural material make great mid-column swing flies. Simply stack mend to get a fly down to the desired depth and begin swinging. Be prepared for many strikes to happen during the final third of the swing as the fly's crosscurrent movement slows. You'll want to assume a casting position that makes sure this latter third of the swing is happening in quality holding water. NATE SIPPLE

rod tip to begin the fight. Because fishing in this fashion usually involves a fair amount of line, and because the smaller rivers on which this technique works best tend to be fairly brushy, it's worth beginning each swing by identifying any nearby obstructions a smallmouth may use to its advantage. Be prepared to fight the fish hard immediately after the hook set, since the angle of battle and direction of current very much favor the fish.

While a floating line, a tapered leader, and an unweighted fly will suffice for most flows, in moderate to broken water, you will need to fish weighted flies, and sometimes even weighted flies on a poly sink tip if you want to get below the surface and stay below the surface for the duration of your swing. Unlike slow spring-creek water, where a fish can move leisurely to inspect a slow-swung fly, in moderate to heavy current we have to be more thoughtful and accurate with both our cast and swing. This means thinking deliberately and strategically about the placement of our feet in the river. A good swung-fly presentation in moderate to heavy flows is one that both begins and ends with the fly in fish-holding water—and hopefully passes over additional fishy water during the middle of the swing. Since the ultimate downstream location is determined by your location in the river, think long and hard about where to position your feet. For instance, positioning yourself in the same current line as a downstream boulder gives you a chance to end your presentation with your fly dangling in a high-percentage zone. Begin your cast in another high-percentage zone, and you've already got two cracks at a good fish with your cast.

Flies for swinging through faster, heavier water should be a bit bulkier than slow-swinging flies, and made with stiffer material. This ensures the fly will maintain a stronger profile in the water without collapsing. Since they are designed to fish in current, many trout-oriented patterns fit this bill nicely, like the Circus Peanut or Sex Dungeon. Articulated patterns can also be pulsed enticingly during the swing and during the dangle. That said, if you are going to use articulated patterns to swing for smallmouth, do yourself and the fish a favor and cut the rear hook. Given the smallmouth's headfirst method of attacking a baitfish, it will only make the process of unhooking fish more difficult.

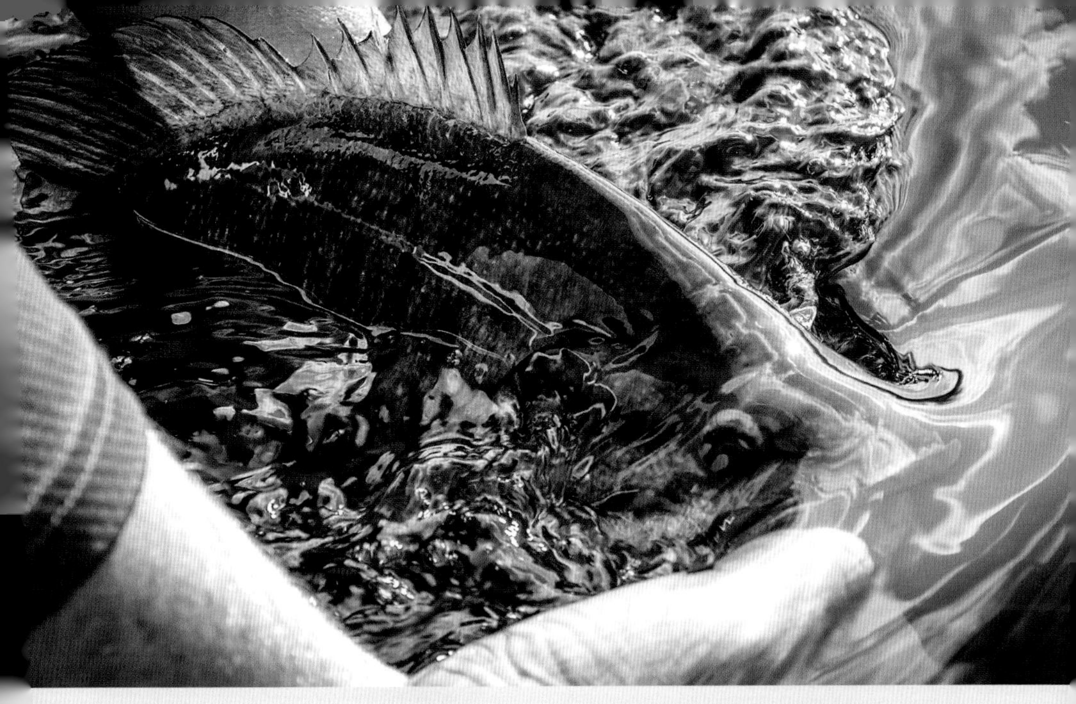

CHAPTER 5

The Lower Column

In structuring this book, one of the things we had to decide on was the order in which we attacked the water column, not as anglers, but as writers. Starting seasonally—beginning and ending with deep-stripping and dredging flies—was one way to go about things, which would have made this chapter first. Instead, we elected to go with a different kind of hierarchy—to begin at the surface and work our way down. Which brings us to the end. In this, our last dedicated presentation chapter, we'll look at several methods for fishing down deep in the water column: deep stripping, deep swinging, and vertical dredging.

While all three methods are about getting and keeping flies in the very lowest portion of the water column, they achieve this in different ways and for different reasons. To distinguish between the approaches in the most basic

As if the challenge and pleasure of fishing smallmouth wasn't enough, they are quite easy on the eyes as well. ERIC CHRISTENSEN

Fishing large flies deep on a sinking line can produce some of the largest fish of the year in the spring and fall. KYLE ZEMPEL

way: 1) Deep stripping is achieved from a moving boat with some sort of sinking line, a short leader, and a heavily dressed weighted fly; 2) deep swinging is achieved from a fixed position (either anchored boat or wading angler) and involves a floating line, a sink tip, and a moderately dressed weighted fly; and 3) deep dredging is performed with indicator-style floating lines, long untapered mono or flouro leaders, and aggressively weighted, lightly dressed flies that get to the bottom fast—and stay there.

The three approaches cover bottom-of-the-column water in different ways. Fished from a moving boat, deep stripping allows us to cover significant water on the x-axis, while vertical dredging allows us to make either long y-axis presentations (one way of thinking about dredging is as the exact inverse of fishing a popper or wiggly) or very short, highly targeted x-axis presentations. Deep swinging achieves a little of both and is best for systematically soaking an area full of known (if lethergic) offenders. But when fish are hunkered close to the river bottom, how do we decide between the three types of presentations? It's a great question with a multifaceted answer. There are different reasons for using each approach, and different conditions as well. Let's look at deep stripping first.

Deep Stripping

Simply put, deep stripping consists of using aggressive sinking lines—either an intermediate line with T-11 or T-14 or sinking lines with aggressive sink rates—coupled with weighted flies that have the size and mass to be noticed down deep, then fishing them back to the boat with a series of strips and pauses. Deep stripping is particularly effective during the cold, often high water of spring, when fish are just starting to become more active but are still in deep water and not looking to move too far, or too fast, for a meal. Deep stripping is distinguished from deep swinging in two ways. First, it allows the angler to cover more river miles, since it's performed from a moving boat. This makes it a good choice for anglers new to a system who are looking to start learning it. Second, and more important, it's the better approach for presenting to holding lies that lie along the x-axis.

When deep stripping, fly design is dictated both by the holding depth and low activity level of the fish. Deep-stripping flies need to get deep and exude passive action during slow strips and the long pauses between strips. Chock-full of meaty natural materials, these flies fish well slow and breathe seductively on the pause. They are heavy in materials because they can afford to be. Deep stripping happens from a moving boat, which means the angler

Top to bottom, left to right: Krakken/Russ Maddin, Red Eye Leech/Mike Schultz, Chicken Changer/Mike Schultz, Mike's Junk Yard Dog/Mike Schmidt, Schultzy's S4 Sculpin/Mike Schultz, Feather Game Changer/Blane Chocklett, Flash Monkey/Russ Maddin, Sex Dungeon/Kelly Galloup, Double Gonga/Charlie Craven, Articulated Leech, Boogie Man/Kelly Galloup, Lazer Sculpin/Charlie Piette. DAVE KARCZYNSKI

is fishing from a raised casting position with a single-handed rod. This allows for relatively easy delivery of a large payload. Natural fur like rabbit strips and wool are often used in deep-stripping flies since they absorb water readily and this absorption helps these flies achieve and maintain depth. Dumbbell and lead barbell eyes are par for the course, and for the dirty water of spring, deep-stripping flies often have larger heads that push water rather than simply slip through it. Do these flies make a loud sound upon landing? Yes they do, but this doesn't usually matter when fish are hunkered down deep in stained water. If anything, the crashing down can serve as an advantage, alerting dormant fish to the arrival of something new into their environment.

In a certain light, deep stripping is a variation of the middle-column streamer fishing that we discussed in the previous chapter, but there are key differences. Middle-column baitfish patterns and retrieves are designed to excite active, metabolically advantaged fish, while deep-stripping patterns are designed to seduce passive, metabolically disadvantaged fish. Color is also a major difference. Because spring water is often off-color, and because deeper water has less light, deep-stripping flies tend to be darker in color and with plenty of darker colored flash (think gold, copper, red), all of which combines to make these flies easier for the fish to see, since darker colors are easier for fish to perceive in more visually compromised environments. The fact that during the early season we're largely imitating leeches, crayfish, sculpins, and other dark-colored prey creatures is another reason deep-stripping flies tend to be darker in color. Once fish become more active and start eating farther up in the column, white again helps the observant angler perceive eats. But until that happens, the smallmouth angler must throw dark flies and rely on his hands, not his eyes, to detect strikes.

Middle-column and bottom-column streamers are also made out of different materials. Highly synthetic flies like some of the middle-column patterns do not necessarily fish well slow—their action is muted, their profile is minimal, their passive action is on the low side, and they don't displace enough water to get noticed in the murky depths. Conversely, deep-stripping flies don't necessarily make good middle-column patterns. They splash down hard, spray water during false casts, are hard to track (because often darker in color), and are prone to snagging in shallow or snaggy water.

Before we move on to tackle for deep stripping, it should be noted that while deep stripping is most commonly practiced during the early conditions of spring, it can also be effective after summertime high-water events when

During high-water conditions, a cushion of soft water typically appears in the vicinity of the bank. Depending on the makeup of the river, this cushion might be a few inches or a few feet. Small cushions are best fished with large, splatting topwater flies. Large cushions are best plied with dark, big-headed sinking flies fished on a sinking line. KYLE ZEMPEL

water clarity is often at a minimum and fish seek refuge in deep slots behind boulders and logjams. Of course, as indicated elsewhere in this book, the first place to explore in a serious midseason high-water event is the first few inches of the bank, and with flies that engage the y-axis, such as large poppers or flashy divers.

Tackle for Deep Stripping

LINES

Deep stripping is the one technique where we opt for dedicated subsurface lines as well as more aggressive weight-forward tapers. These weight-forward tapers make sense because deep stripping represents the least refined presentation method: We aren't doing much aerial or on-the-water mending, nor are we overly concerned with landing the fly gently. We also tend to be fishing a little closer to the fish. All of this means that an aggressive weight-forward line makes a lot of sense. In an aggressive shooting-head-style line, the bulk of the line's mass is located at the front of the head, and the belly and rear taper are

One of the foodstuffs deep-stripping flies imitate is the sculpin. ERIC CHRISTENSEN

nearly nonexistent. These lines are often referred to as shooting heads since they are not made to be aerialized, but rather shot after a crisp double haul (and minimal false casting). Attempting to aerialize rabbit strip leeches with lead dumbbell eyes is not only miserable, it's downright dangerous.

As for sink rate, the right line for your deep-stripping needs might be an intermediate line (with a sink rate of one to two inches per second) for smaller, shallower rivers, a type vi sinking line (with a sink rate of six to eight inches per second) for larger rivers and bigger flows, or something in between—a type 3 sinking line. Not looking to carry so many different lines? The most versatile setup would be an intermediate line coupled with a sink tip of a length and density appropriate for the day's conditions. Level sink tips like T-8, T-11, or T-14 get you down fastest when surface slap is not a problem, whereas poly tips (which are tapered and therefor allow for more elegant and controlled presentations) might be a better choice when presentations must be more subtle. Another difference between level tips and poly tips is that level tips are easier to customize and experiment with. Simply chop them up in the desired length, right down to one or two feet. If you do this with a poly tip, you are essentially losing its primary feature—its taper. Whether you go with poly tips or level tips or both, an intermediate line and array of tips is a good choice for anglers with rivers with variable terrain, where you might be fishing long mid-depth flats one minute and sudden deeper pools the next. Plus, if fish end up being closer to the surface, simply get rid of the tips altogether and voilá—you're fishing just below the film.

RODS

While in previous chapters we talked about six, seven, and eight weights, here we are going to come straight out and say that an eight weight is going to make your life much easier and more manageable. Beyond that, if you're interested in learning this style of fishing and fishing it well, a fast-action rod is the way to go. Fast-action rods make lifting a heavy, waterlogged fly and a length of sink tip out of the water much easier. They also make steering these rigs over and around structure more efficient, since the rod doesn't bend as much. If you really do prefer a slower rod, and do intend to go with one of the more aggressively tapered shooting lines we've been discussing, you might consider underlining your rod by one line size.

LEADERS

Leaders for deep stripping are simple and come in two flavors: short and long. A shorter leader—say, two feet—will get your fly down immediately but achieve less depth over the course of a retrieve. Short leaders are best when presentations are relatively short and you need to start fishing immediately. A longer leader of five-plus feet will take a bit longer to get to depth, but it will achieve a deeper ultimate depth. These longer leaders are best when making long casts over large, deep water where you need your fly to keep gaining depth as it makes its way back to the boat.

What does this look like in practice? When you know you'll be mostly pounding the bank and fishing the first shelf, as might be the case in high water with fish holding close to the bank, go with as short of a leader as you can get away with. For fishing the second shelf and mid-river structure, err on the longer side of things (but be sure to cast far beyond your target zone and give your fly time to get to depth).

On a related note, think of your leader length as something to experiment with if you find yourself fishing too shallow or too deep for conditions—controlling depth is much more than just opting for a more heavily weighted fly (and vice versa). If you're scraping bottom, shorten your leader. And if you're running too high over the holes, lengthen it.

Fishing Deep-Stripping Rigs

The first part of any presentation is the cast, and casting shooting-head-type lines is a little different if you're coming from, say, the world of trout fishing with a conventionally tapered floating line. Like spey lines, shooting lines are designed to cast best with a fixed amount of line out—the head. If you have too much running line out, you will quickly find yourself without a way to transfer the energy of the rod through the running line and into the cast. Running line, being limp and thin, is a poor conductor of energy. Most modern shooting lines are equipped with a color change to help anglers locate the transition point where the head meets the running line. Experiment with your casting stroke and pay attention to how your casting responds to various launch points within two to three feet on either side of the transition.

These should be cast with a roll-cast pickup or a water load. You'll quickly learn what you and your rod are capable of picking up out of the water as you set up to recast. We've seen many anglers attempt to pick up a sinking line/fly way too early and just about throw their shoulder out trying to get it out of the water. In the case of a dark fly, it's tough to see until it gets right on the rod tip. We tell our clients to strip until they hear the "tick" of the fly line/leader knot come to the rod tip.

So you've got the line in the air. Now what? With a conventionally tapered floating line, you could feed line into your false casting to carry more and

While they require more physical effort than throwing poppers, fishing deep-stripping flies on a sinking line is the most effective way to fish when your fly needs to be both on the bottom and swimming along the x-axis. Eliminating any and all unnecessary motions from your casting stroke will help prevent early fatigue. NATE SIPPLE

more line in the air, and lengthen your cast that way. This just doesn't work with shooting-head-type lines—your cast will collapse. As such, we're looking to single or double haul these lines, again, paying particular attention to the launch point.

If we were going to summarize the steps of casting a shooting-head-type line, we'd do so in four steps: 1) Complete your retrieve; 2) perform a roll cast or water load to get the shooting head out of your guide; 3) if necessary, false cast once to get the desired amount of line out; 4) double haul and launch.

BOAT CONTROL

Now that we've covered delivery, let's talk about the other presentation variable when it comes to deep stripping: boat control. Boat control is particularly important when deep stripping, since so much of the action of the fly depends on the passive materials during the between-strip swoons. Between strips we really want the fly to hang there in the current without too much drag. Especially when we're talking about longer-tailed streamers and articulated streamers, much of the action happens during the stop, the pause, the recovery. While it might only last a fraction of a second, it's in that second half of the stripping equation that an articulated fly can kick its rear portions out and away from the head of the fly and do its best impression of floundering food, or for a long rabbit-fur tail to flail fetchingly in the current. The key to keeping that action going is to avoid dampening, and dampening comes from drag. In the case of sinking lines fishing from a moving boat, drag comes from moving either slower or faster than the current. Go too slow and your line will bow downstream of the boat, pulling the fly forward when it should be recovering. Go too fast and it'll be the boat, and not the current, pulling the fly downstream. In both cases the end result is the same: a streamer that doesn't swim nearly as well as it should.

So how do you solve this problem? By communicating with the guy or gal on the sticks. Mind you, this is a lot easier when you're fishing with a regular partner. During the fall a friend of Dave's wondered aloud why they tended to be so successful when fishing together. The best answer they could come up with was they were comfortable enough to bark at each other if the boat was moving in a way that didn't complement the other's fishing. What might have looked like verbal abuse from the outside was really just the best kind of streamer teamwork.

So now we know that in general we want the fly to be moving at about the speed of the boat, and the boat to be just a hair slower than the current—just enough to give you some steering control. Technically we *could* accomplish that by casting directly perpendicular from the boat. But deep stripping has a special challenge that affects how far in front of the boat we fish, and that

Fishing in front of the boat is key for several reasons. For one, it is easy to gain extra depth: Simply throw a upstream mend and let the fly fall on a slack line. Second, and more important, the motion of a fly "falling back into the fish," as Michigan guide Mike Schultz puts it, tends to be what activates the interest and hunger of early and late-season bass. MICHAEL LESCHISIN

challenge is strike detection. Deep stripping is one of the few techniques with absolutely no visual element to the eat. There's no line to watch, no indicator to be seen, no flash of fish to tell you you've been attacked. Instead, all you've got is feel, and, especially early and late in the year, that feel can be mushy. Fish in cold water tend to take the fly *much* more subtly than they do in the warmer months, and this soft eat is further complicated by the fact that fish in cold water tend to "eat and keep coming," by which we mean they will swim toward deep water after chowing down, which is usually smack in the direction of the boat. The slack this creates not only hides your ability to feel the take, but also obstructs your ability to set the hook. And so our position of the fly relative to the boat becomes a central issue. Thus: When deep stripping, it's very important to fish out in front of the boat.

Fishing out in front of the boat has several key advantages. First, it improves your angle on the hook set—a fish is not coming at you, it's more coming across you, so by performing a solid strip set followed by an upstream line sweep, we have a good chance of sticking our fish.

Sticking the fish is one thing, but fighting a fish coming at you is quite another. Many experienced fly anglers fish with us each year, but some of them do not have any experience with river smallmouth bass. Anglers that fish from drift boats for trout have a completely different technique for landing trout than we do fishing smallmouth. When a trout is hooked from a boat, most times the fish will take up the slack and move downstream, creating a tight line from the fish to the reel. At this time the angler can fight the fish comfortably from the reel and use the mechanical or manual drag to his advantage. The true difference between a smallmouth and a trout is the trout is a sprinter and a smallmouth is a street fighter. This is incredibly important to understand when fighting smallmouth. If you wait for the bass to pull the line tight and make a run, you are sure to lose the fish. The truth is that you should absolutely never fight a bass on the reel. By the time a smallmouth would get to the reel he would have thrown the hook. We call them street fighters because they run to a safe area and then try to beat you up in close quarters. This is the reason to set the hook and strip like crazy until it feels like you are going to break it off.

RETRIEVES

Retrieves are terrifically important when deep stripping. In fact, because of the variability in the mood of fish during the deep-stripping time of year (usually the early season), no other technique requires as much experimentation. One retrieve might garner reactions while another might have no effect at all. And the preferred retrieve may change over the course of a weekend or even a single fishing day. This is where it can be helpful to fill the boat to max angling capacity. With two casting anglers in the boat, each can experiment with different retrieves until finding something that works. What about when only one angler is casting? One early season tip is to vary your retrieve *every cast* as a way to apprehend the bass's mood on a given day of fishing. There are, in fact, a good number of retrieves you can come up with. Pick three to four and cycle through them in three to four cast sequences. Short strips with short pauses. Long strips with long pauses. Short strips with long pauses. Long strips with short pauses. Steady strips and erratic strips. The list of possible retrieves and retrieve combinations within a single cast is long. Cycling through them will help you to figure out the ideal retrieve for a given day. And varying your retrieve every cast can help you get dialed into the day's preferred retrieve faster than, say, changing your retrieve every fifteen minutes. If it's your third retrieve that is the bread-and-butter retrieve of the day and you only discover this after forty-five minutes of fishing, you've just wasted close to an hour of fishing. When deep stripping in early spring, change your retrieve before you change your fly. And remember, the *fish will* change their moods and behaviors throughout the day. Just because something worked on a few fish between eleven o'clock and noon does not mean that it will work on fish from two to four in the afternoon. If you think you figured the day out but hit a slow patch of action midday, go into retrieve-experimentation mode. Subtle changes in the water temps, lighting, or prey activity can all change the way fish will act (and react) to flies.

An early season bass heads back to its deepwater resting lie. ERIC CHRISTENSEN

Deep Swinging

Swinging flies slowly just above the bottom can be an effective early season technique when fish are hunkered down deep, but it can also be effective during the summer on deeper flats (three to five feet) when fish have lock-jaw midday and nothing seems to work. In both cases, we tend to be looking at slower current flows, so we want to take some cues from steelhead swing culture when building or modifying flies.

Steelhead swingers know that different material responds differently to current. Some fibers, like marabou, craft fur, rabbit fur, schlappen, fine rubber legs, Finn raccoon, and fine-gauged flash move well in slow current—that's because their fibers are fine and limp and responsive to slight amounts of current. But put those same fibers into faster flows and they collapse, losing their profile and much of their action. In faster flows, stiffer and more robust materials like deer hair, arctic fox, larger gauge flash, various synthetics, stout rubber legs, and stiff-stemmed saddle hackle are better choices.

In the case of deep swinging for smallmouth bass, we are generally looking for flies that derive their action from some combination of limp materials. In general, we've found that darker patterns make better deeply fished flies, so leech-, sculpin-, and crayfish-inspired patterns all make for good deep-swinging flies. Many of the flies we've already discussed in this section make good deep-swinging flies.

The finer points of deep swinging are dependent on depth, current, and fish location, so we'll deal with cold-water deep swinging (which tends to happen in deeper and slower flows) and warm-water deep swinging (which happens shallower and in moderate flows) separately. Let's start by talking about early spring.

Early season deep swinging is most often done from boats, for the simple reason that in the spring fish are hunkered down in deep water, and it's just too difficult (or dangerous) to wade into appropriate positions. That's largely because when we swing flies, we are trying to position ourselves so the end of the swing (generally refered to as the "hang down" part of the swing) puts our fly in the very best water. In early spring, "hang down" is probably happening in water at least six feet deep, and if we're standing anywhere near that, wading is simply not possible. Instead, fishing from an anchored boat gives us the best shot at presenting to early season fish. Boats should be anchored on the edge of the seam—where the soft holding water of early spring meets main flows—and hang down should happen just on the soft, inside edge of this seam.

In deep swinging, the name of the game is to fish as deeply as possible without hanging up. And there are four factors that affect your depth: density of

Natural materials and articulation are deadly when it comes to deep swinging. When fishing early and late-season lies, no quality holding water should be abandoned until it's seen several quality swings. COREY HASELHUHN

your tip (whether T-8, T-11, or T-14), length of your tip, weight of your fly, and mending. Within those parameters, there are changes we can make to affect the depth and path of our fly, but the easiest would definitely be mending. Simply put, an upstream mend will gain you depth and slow your swing, while a downstream mend will lose you depth (and quicken your swing). Depending on the size and shape of your lie, and the presence or absence of structure, you may find yourself upstream mending early in the swing to get down to depth and downstream mending if you're scraping bottom or simply want to accelerate the fly.

Whereas swinging flies for top-column and middle-column smallies was more similar to classical trout swinging, deep swinging takes its cues from the cold-weather swing culture of steelhead anglers. There are a few reasons for this. In the previous chapters, the speed of our presentations was determined by the location and mood of our fish. If bass are going to chase a swung fly up top, it's because they are in an ultra-aggressive mood, and a faster swing is more likely to garner a response: No need to mend, just cast and hold on. The same is mostly true for swinging up middle-column fish. We are appealing to actively feeding fish in obvious feeding lies, places where moderate to quick current flows come up against some sort of seam, though it's also true that swinging middle-column leechy patterns also appeals to neutral fish. In both of the

Dave Whitlock's Near Nuff crayfish family of flies are great for slow swinging over mid-depth flats.
DAVE KARCZYNSKI

above cases, our line management is at a relative minimum. Because we don't need to get the fly down to terrific depth, we don't need to stack mend prior to the swing. And because our fish are aggressively feeding, we don't need to slow the rate of the swing; thus the angle of our rod relative to our line as we fish through the swing is not a life-or-death issue. Lastly, because we don't need several yards of river to get down to presentation depth, the "fishing" part of the cast begins the moment the fly hits the water with top- and middle-column swinging. But when the situation calls for deep swinging, we're looking at a very different presentation. If we have to resort to fishing close to the bottom, it's usually because fish are in an inactive mood. Moving slowly is the key to fishing. And getting deep and moving slowly means not only fishing high-grain weight heads (Skagit heads, scandi heads, or simply a weight-forward floating line overweighted by two to three rod weights) and sink tips, but thinking of the presentation in two different parts: the "getting down deep" part of the cast, where mending and line manipulation gain both depth and a straight-line connection to the fly, and the "fishing" part of the cast—"the swing."

First off, we need to give our flies time to get down to depth, so the point at which the fly lands and the point at which we begin fishing the swing are not the same thing. Just how high above the fishing water you need to cast will depend on depth and flows.

The first thing to focus on is the angle of the cast. Rather than casting at a forty-five-degree angle to the bank, your cast should be closer to ninety degrees, or straight across. Advanced casters will want to perform an aerial reach mend to lay the floating portion of the swing rig upstream, thus allowing the fly and sink tip to fall on a relatively slack line. Beginning casters will want to cast and throw a quick upstream mend. Whether the mend happens in the air or on the water, the more upstream mending you do, the greater the depth you'll achieve.

The second step before preparing to fish the swing is coming tight to the fly. With your rod stuck at an angle (this is where a longer rod comes in handy), stop the fly, establish a direct connection (one without a bow or slack), and begin a controlled swing. Your rod is guiding the fly, but it's doing so by following it slowly. By doing this we have a more or less straight line to the fly, which aids in strike detection.

Special note: If you will be deep wading, be sure to exercise caution. It's advisable to fish these techniques in water you either know well or can otherwise be certain is safe. The weather of the early season is often powerful and turbid, making sharp drops, midstream boulders, and other potentially dangerous obstacles quite possible. The water is also cold. We don't want you to take a swim. For these presentations, we recommend waders and sturdy wading boots with stud or cleat reinforcements. A collapsible wading staff is advocated. Fish water you know well, and don't take risks.

BOTTOM-COLUMN SWINGING DURING THE SUMMER

While not the most dynamic of presentations, deep swinging to neutral summer fish on the edge between the first and second shelf, through pockets and holes, and across mid-depth flats, can save the day when nothing else is working. In fact, by using this technique Dave experienced the best smallmouth fishing of his life between one and three o'clock in the afternoon on a day when nothing and no one else could get a fish. Enticing these negative fish means fishing your slowest swing possible and relying on the passive action of your materials to entice a take. These are subtle takes. We've found darker colors with some sort of "hot spot" or stark contrast to be very effective. Black and tan, black and olive, and black and orange are effective combinations.

Bottom-column swinging during the summer doesn't require much specialty gear to accomplish, though a long rod does aid in controlling the swing. As far as sink tip goes, a poly leader will allow you a more refined presentation than a level sink tip. They make sense because you won't be fishing too terribly deep—usually at three to five feet—and a subtler presentation will be more useful than a clumsy one.

Swinging deep should by no means be limited to cold water early and late in the summer. Slow swinging crayfish patterns over deeper flats on hot summer afternoons can turn a slow day into a slamming one. HEIDI OBERSTADT

RODS FOR BOTTOM-COLUMN SWINGING

While an indicator or switch rod in the ten- to eleven-foot class is an ideal tool for this type of fishing, it's nonetheless also possible with a nine-foot rod and an overweighted floating line.

Dredging

Pop quiz: If 90 percent of a smallmouth's diet is crayfish, and crayfish spend 100 percent of their time on the bottom, why are we saving vertical dredging, that most crayfishy of presentations, for the last part of the last presentation chapter of this book?

There are a couple of reasons. First off, as we've established throughout this book, even when smallmouth are keyed in on crayfish they are absolutely amenable to other prey opportunities. *Micropterus dolomieu* is an opportunistic feeder in ways that trout are not. Even though smallmouth bass may often align their habitat where crayfish are abundant, that doesn't mean that they are not always ready for a non-crayfish opportunity. One of the sayings we've talked about time and again is that opportunity trumps quantity, opportunity trumps quantity, opportunity trumps quantity. So even as a given fish might be cruising a shallow, rocky flat with a daily lunch of crustaceans on the mind, when presented with the opportunity to pluck a twitching morsel from the surface, or to crush an injured minnow, it's more than happy to do so. It's happened dozens of time where we'll be guiding clients and encounter an amazing drake hatch. A visibly concerned trout angler will turn to us and ask why we're fishing a chartreuse popper and not trying to match the hatch. "Curiosity killed the cat" is our reply. And curiosity gets the better of smallmouth as well. Why they eat certain foods when nothing else like it is in the water is a mystery when you compare it to trout, but not so much a mystery when you compare it to a human being. Even if you enjoyed and were accustomed to eating a six-inch cold cut sub sandwich every day for a year, if a big T-bone with a twice-baked potato plopped down in front of you, you wouldn't hesitate to pick up a knife and fork. Smallmouth, in this way, are a lot like us.

This leads us to our second reason for placing dredging here at the back. As you've probably noticed by now, much of this book is concerned less about flies as a foodstuff and more about flies as a presentation technology. A wiggly can fish in places and in ways a crayfish just can't. Take the case of a smallmouth laid up in water barely covering its back. That opportunistic fish would

Meaty, buggy, and with plenty of plummeting weight: These are the three primary characteristics of a good dredging fly. Reverse-tied hooks are an essential part of the dredging game. You'll still hang up from time to time, but those hang-ups will tend to be less fatal to your hook points. Still, be sure to carry a hook hone and make regular use of it when bumping flies along the bottom. HEIDI OBERSTADT

probably just as equally eat a natural damselfly, sculpin, or crayfish. But when it comes to presenting imitations of those foodstuffs, our options suddenly become quite limited. Plopping a rabbit-fur and lead crayfish imitation or even a baitfish is more likely to scare the bejesus out of that fish than get it to eat. But lay a wiggly delicately upstream on a reach cast, let it float along the y-axis to the fish, and bend its legs ever so slightly, and you've got more than a good chance of a rendezvous with a bass.

That said, sometimes we absolutely need to present slow, deep, and on the y-axis. Say we're fishing deep shelves in the early season where fish are hanging right around the break. At such a time dredging gives our flies the best chance for getting—and staying—in front of a fish's face.

So let's get to talking about getting down and dirty—bouncing baits off the very bottom of the river. What is vertical dredging, exactly? And how does it differ from deep stripping?

Simply put, deep stripping allows you to fish near the bottom as you retrieve the fly perpendicular to the current—that is, stripping back toward the boat. This works great when fish-holding lies tend to fall along the x-axis, or where woody debris is abundant. But if fish are oriented along y-axis structure, then

This dredged summer fish came off an edge where the second shelf meets the main river channel. With two anglers in the boat, try to position watercraft so that each angler can fish a different y-axis edge. NATE SIPPLE

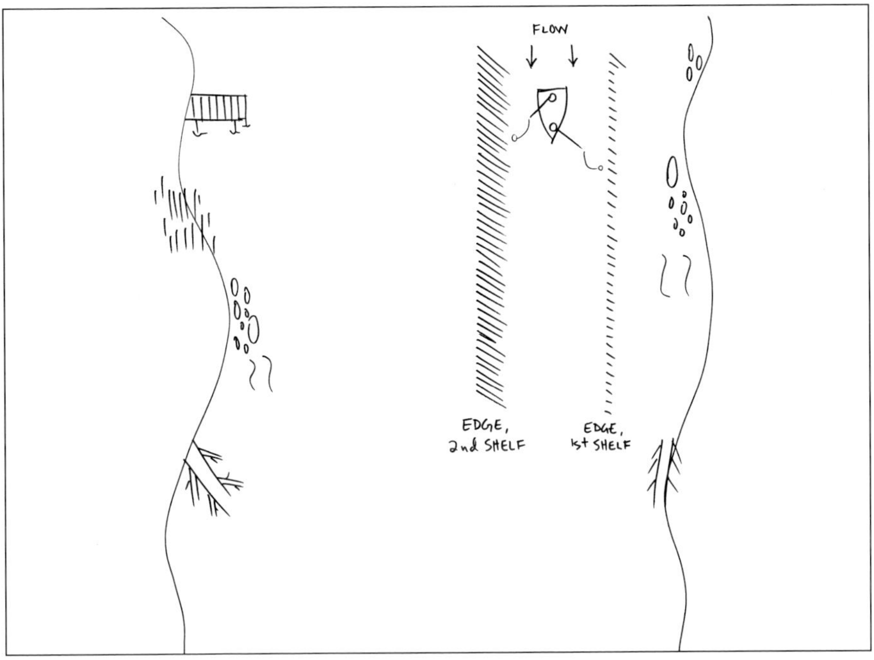

When two anglers are vertical dredging, the angler at the front of the boat should tackle the edge between the first and second shelf, while the rear angler should tackle the edge where the second shelf meets the deepest part of the river channel. Deeper water fish are less likely to be spooked by a boat passing overhead. DAVE KARCZYNSKI

deep stripping is only going to put the fly in a bass's face for a relatively short amount of time. Dredging, conversely, puts the fly on the bottom and moves with the current, parallel to the bank, from either an anchored or moving boat.

So, when do we dredge? First off, vertical dredging is a great way to roll when water temperatures are anywhere below fifty degrees and fish are hunkered down in deep pockets. These metabolically disadvantaged fish are not going to move far for a fly, and they aren't going to go after something that looks like it wants to be chased. That's the situation a smallmouth bass finds itself in during its months of dormancy: open to easy opportunity, but acutely aware that any expenditure of energy not without guarantee of remuneration is unwise. To gain a better idea of what severe metabolic disadvantage feels like, imagine your body the first seconds after waking up in the morning. If a piece of bacon sidles up to your nightstand, great; you might reach out and pop it in your mouth. But you're probably not going to chase an omelet down the stairs.

But vertical dredging isn't only for early and late in the season. There are also those days where fish aren't looking up and aren't interested in giving chase. You'll know those days when you stumble upon them. Fishing should

Oxygen levels are at their lowest midsummer, so use tackle that ensures your battles with fish are as brief as possible. MICHAEL LESCHISIN

be good, but it simply isn't. Surface and middle-column baits aren't producing. The answer is a floating line (with or without an indicator within a foot of the line tip), an aggressively weighted, lightly dressed fly, and a straight mono or fluoro leader. The fly is cast out, allowed to sink on or very near the bottom, and then drifted along with bumps.

As the illustration on the previous page suggests, one way of deploying deep dredging is with the front angler fishing the second shelf while the first angler fishes the first shelf. Doing this can help figure out where the fish are active and what they are likely to be eating on a given day. Another way to deploy deep dredging is if you pick up a fish deep stripping early or late in the season. Mark the spot, back off from it, anchor upstream, and make a few dredging presentations through the general area. Where there's one early season fish, there's likely more.

Vertical dredging can increase the chances of presenting a fly to deep-dwelling but catchable fish—if you do it right. One important part of vertical dredging is to know the depth of the water you're presenting to. If you're trying to reach fish sulking on bottom structure but your fly is only in the middle of the column, you aren't reaching those fish. This means that with dredging we either need to be fishing uniform water (such as a shelf) or be prepared to make depth adjustments regularly through the use of an indicator.

Vertical dredging is a great technique to use when you've caught a fish and want to really soak the surrounding water. If you're having a slow day and take a fish on a minnow pattern, it's time to drop anchor and focus: Where there is one smallmouth, there is likely more. On more than one occasion, 90 percent of our fish on a guide trip came while the boat was anchored. This is especially true on difficult days, which are more common early and late in the season but also show up from time to time in late spring and early summer. At such times positioning the boat in likely areas is paramount, as is working the spot slowly and thoroughly. When fish are deep and grouped up in five to ten feet of water, they can be almost fished off the end of the oar with success. At such times, shorter casts also allow us to detect strikes better, as well as control the depth and speed of the fly.

Next, since vertical dredging is essentially the inverse of popper fishing (both allow you to fish y-axis structure effectively, with one at the surface and the other at the bottom), vertical dredging is an excellent technique for presenting to fish on a deeper second shelf on an y-axis stretch of river. With smart mending and strategic boat control, you can keep your fly ticking along the bottom in the zone for a good while, in much the same way a well-drifted wiggly can do so up top.

Vertical dredging, though, isn't always an y-axis presentation. In some cases, larger eddy systems mean there just isn't an even flow to ride. In other

When fishing still water, the only route a fly can take is straight back to the boat. Fishing weighted flies vertically with an untapered leader can allow you to vertically jig at a distance. On clear flats, this approach allows you to sight-fish to moody bass hunkered down on the bottom. LUKE KAVAJECZ

cases, there may be no flow at all (early and late in the season). In such cases, we don't have the option of dead-drifting with a bump. Instead, we twitch the fly forward, pausing between twitches to let the fly settle back to the bottom. This method of pulling the fly through the water doesn't keep us in the zone quite as effectively as with drifting along the y-axis, but it's the next best thing.

Dredging Lines and Rigging

Most people thing that the way to get down the deepest and fastest is to use an aggressive sinking line. While these lines are great for stripping streamers at depth, when we want to dredge they quickly become the poorest of tools. That's because these lines are much, much thicker than monofilament, so immediately we are dealing with drag. And in the swirling, uneven currents that we invariably have to negotiate when fishing the bottom of the water column, they are just a bad idea.

Sinking lines aren't ideal for another reason. And that's because once the line gets down, it stays down, catching on boulders and trees and such. When dredging, we definitely don't want our line or leader on the bottom, where all the snags are. We just want our fly there.

This is a fact: When it comes to getting the deepest fastest—and staying there—there's absolutely no substitute for a thin, untapered leader on a floating line. We tend to favor indicator-style floating lines for this type of fishing (extrabouyant heads float the line high in the water, and the high visibility aids in strike detection). We also make regular use of small stick-on-type strike indicators. They're small, cheap, and don't hinder casting at all. That subtle pickup can be very difficult to detect if you're not used to seeing it. A small indicator can save the day if situations call for going low and slow.

Let's talk more about the dredging leader. If you're new to fly fishing and have spent countless hours trying to understand leader taper, our recommendation is either going to liberate you or frustrate you. But an untapered leader is really the way to go if you want to dredge effectively. Vertical dredging is also the one occasion we see for using fluorocarbon as the primary leader material, as it has a better diameter/strength ratio and a different density in the water. We're not fond of its environmental drawbacks, but thankfully we're usually not using much more than ten to twelve feet at a time. It also has a low stretch coefficient, which is a big deal when the fly is way down on the bottom and you have to drive home a 1/0 hook.

Whether stripping baitfish patterns or ticking weighted patterns along the bottom, bass fishing success begins with good line management. NATE SIPPLE

Our realization of the power of untapered mono and fluoro leaders came as a result of much empirical experimentation. Many years ago we rented out a swimming pool, put on scuba masks, and experimented with all types of flies, lines, and leaders. And while it was true that different flies sank at different speeds, we realized that a far more significant coefficient was line and leader. It definitely wasn't a combination of T-14 and a weight fly that went down the fastest. Instead, it was the combination of a floating line, weighted fly, and untapered leader. And the difference wasn't even subtle. When we put a tapered leader on, the sink rate was half. It was a huge difference. A tapered leader parachutes the fly, whereas ten feet of straight, untapered tippet literally razors through the water column.

Is this an easy rig to cast? Certainly not at first. But, like anything out there, once you get the hang of it with a modified stroke, it isn't all that bad. Again, minimalizing false casts, keeping your loops wide and loose, and knowing your limitations are key. And don't be afraid to backhand or water load if need be. The fish don't care how the fly gets there nearly as much as we do. Don't worry about how pretty it is; just deliver the meal to the door. As an added bonus, the dredging technique allows you to reposition with mends once you deliver your payload anyway. Fish are going to be down deep: They won't mind your on-the-water adjustments to a sloppy cast.

Before we get down to the presentation techniques for fishing vertical dredgers, let's take a look at the flies themselves.

Dredging Flies

Lead dumbbell eyes. Tungsten heads. Metal coneheads. Lead wraps. One thing dredging flies have in common is that they possess one or more plummeting agents. While deep-stripping flies typically seek to have "just enough weight" to get down with a sinking line, dredging flies are born to fall. But weight is not the only thing that affects sink rate. The materials with which they are made also make a huge difference with how fast a fly falls and how easily it stays at depth. Sparsely dressed flies full of limp fibers definitely make the best dredging flies. The most effective dredging flies are those that attain bulk and action using only the bare minimum materials to do so. We still want to get our flies noticed and for them to be enticing, but we also want to make sure we can control our flies at depth, that the current is not kiting our flies away from us.

Whenever possible, dredging flies employ synthetic materials that give body to natural materials to create the illusion of bulk without actual bulk. This is particularly relevant in terms of palmered body materials and undercollars.

Top to bottom, left to right: Clouser Deep Minnow/Bob Clouser, Coffey's Sparkle Minnow/Greg Coffey, Critter Craw/Chuck Kraft, Rabbit Strip Sculpin, Mud Bug/Nelson Ham, Autumn Splendor/Tim Hang, Grim Reaper/Pat Ehlers, Moppet/Tim Landwehr, Near 'Nuff Crayfish/ Dave Whitlock, Meat Whistle/John Barr, Hairy Fodder/Craig Riendeau, Bighorn Bugger, Murdich Wiggler/Bill Murdich, Critter Mite/Chuck Kraft. DAVE KARCZYNSKI

Dredging patterns can also be fished from a wading position, though drifts will invariably be shorter. Extend your presentation by allowing your dredged fly to swing upward on a taut line at the end of your drift. NATE SIPPLE

There are a variety of great "brushes" on the market that build body and add flash at the same time. Where we do employ natural materials, we look to apply minimal amounts and via intelligent methods. Furs found on the hide can be put into dubbing loops to form collars. Flies tied via dubbing loops maintain all the action of, say, rabbit fur, but do so without creating bulk, which would slow the descent of a fly and allow it to sail upwards too much upon manipulation in current. As you're probably sensing by now, you have to find that perfect balance between movement and a fly that has a slim enough profile to fall in the water column to create the ideal dredger. The Barr's Meat Whistle is a perfect example of this. You have the natural movement and undulation of the marabou, but it's simple and slim enough that it falls nicely in the water. By contrast, the Tequeely (which we discussed in the previous chapter) and its profile do not make it a good candidate for a fast-sinking fly.

Last but not least, many dredging flies are either tied on sixty- or ninety-degree jig hooks or weighted in such a way as to reverse the ride of the hook. This eliminates the chances of the fly hanging on the bottom and improves hookup percentages. The Meat Whistle, Menominee Mudbug, and Hairy Fodder are examples of this style. Even so, when you tie dredgers, tie a few extra—if you are fishing these flies correctly, you will lose more than a few.

When tying these patterns, we recommend doing so in different weight classes. For instance, you might tie a Meat Whistle in several configurations—with a brass cone, a tungsten cone, brass dumbbell eyes, lead dumbbell eyes, or a Sculpin Helmet. I like to vary the weight by tying some with brass dumbbells and some with tungsten.

Walleye anglers who vertically fish jigs off the bottom know the importance of having the right amount of weight for the job. Too much weight and your jig lags far behind the boat, where it gets pulled off the bottom and upwards in the column. In which case you've lost contact with fish holding close to the river bottom, and you are at more of an awkwardly angled connection to your fly.

Too little weight creates the opposite problem—a fly that gets snatched by the current and carried downstream. The situation is the same, however: an angler at a severe angle to a fly riding several feet above where you want it.

It will take some practice properly triangulating river depth, current speed, and fly weight. Getting the right weight is very important. When your fly is hanging more or less vertically beneath the tip of your fly line, you're fishing at your deepest. You also have the most direct connection to the fly. One long strip to remove activity from the fly paired with the raising of the rod tip is all it takes.

The Art of Vertical Dredging

The hardest part of dredging flies is not necessarily fishing them, but fishing them *well.* For all their benefits, there are some inherent difficulties in fishing vertical dredgers, starting with connection to the fly.

Fishing topwater flies, you can see the fish eat your fly. Fishing in the middle of the column takes a little more work, you see and/or feel it. And when deep stripping there's generally some sort of hard or soft tug. None of these cues is available to the dredging angler. At best, there's the tip of the fly line—or an indicator—to watch. It's here that we give credit to one of smallmouth fishing's great innovators, Minnesota guide and author Tim Holschlag, whose books on bass were truly groundbreaking. Tim realized that even experienced anglers simply couldn't detect the strike of the smallmouth fast enough to capitalize on it, and that the indicator could make it far easier for the angler.

Vertical dredging from a moving boat requires the angler and rower to be on the same page. Here Bart Landwehr checks the position of his client's indicator to make sure the boat is running just a bit slower than the current. This will put the fly downstream of the boat and introduce a gentle belly in the line that will help bump the fly downstream instead of straight back to the boat. NAPE SIPPLE

Dredging is best practiced from a boat moving roughly the same speed as the current. Simply cast your fly, put a slight downstream belly in the fly line (the fly should be drifting just a few feet downstream of the angler's position in the boat), and add occasional bumps to entice fish and avoid hanging up. Less is definitely more when it comes to manipulating any dredging fly: Too much stripping, mending, or twitching will pull it up and out of the bottom twelve inches of the water column, which is *exactly* where we want it. For strike detection, watch for the tip of the fly line—we like trouty indicator lines for this technique since they tend to have brightly colored, extra bouyant tips (try waxing the tips with some high-floatant paste for even more buoyancy). When the line stops, darts off to the side, or turns upstream, it's time to set the hook.

As diagrammed below, we fish vertical-dredging flies at a near-ninety-degree angle that is just downstream of the boat, with a belly in the line. That belly in the line ensures that when we do manipulate the fly, it moves downstream, not straight back to the boat, which would be very unnatural and which would also pull it across current—and therefore upward in the

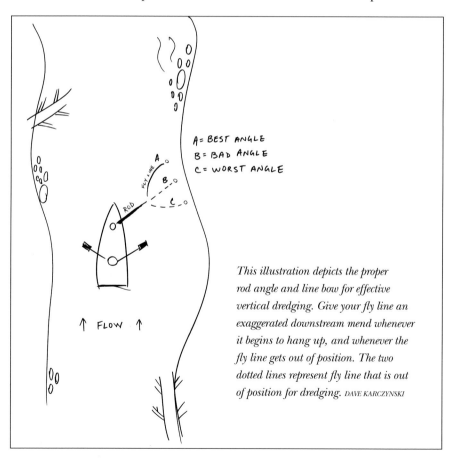

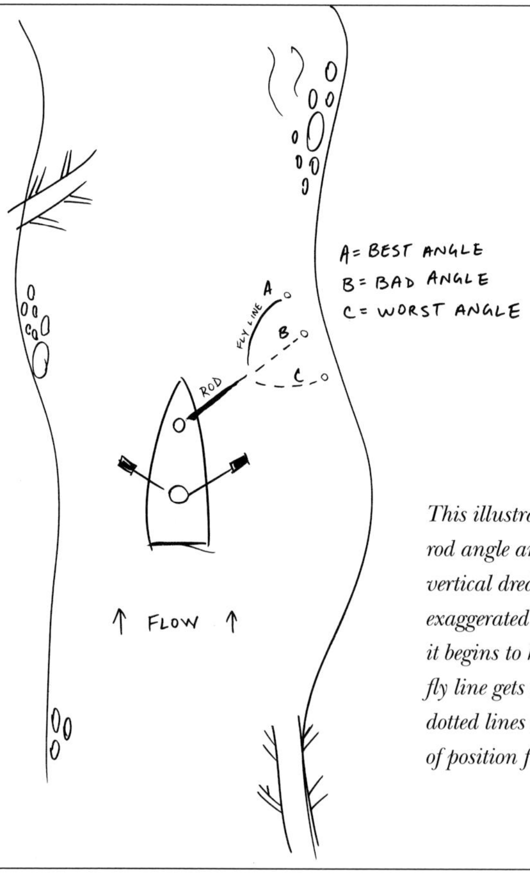

This illustration depicts the proper rod angle and line bow for effective vertical dredging. Give your fly line an exaggerated downstream mend whenever it begins to hang up, and whenever the fly line gets out of position. The two dotted lines represent fly line that is out of position for dredging. DAVE KARCZYNSKI

With the rod tucked below his armpit, rod pointing down at the water, and line hand at the ready, Tim Landwehr is in perfect position to set the hook. When dredging, this will consist of a strip to pick up slack line in the belly followed by a sharp upward rod snap. HEIDI OBERSTADT

water column. Because at this point your leader will be entirely underwater, the only thing we can really watch is the line tip. Now that we've got this fly down to depth, how do we work it?

In the early days of fishing for smallmouth, the idea was to simply imitate nymphing for trout but on a slightly larger scale—say, with beadhead Woolly Buggers. And it works some of the time. Fish a bugger on an indicator in the right water and you'll pick up a few fish. But you can do much, much better, because fundamentally smallmouth aren't like trout, which wait for a nymph to come rolling by their holding lie on the bottom. Smallmouth bass respond to movement. And so we need to "bump" our dredged fly.

If the basic presentation unit of the topwater fly was "the pop," and the basic unit of the middle-column baitfish was "the strip," then the basic presentation unit of the dredger is "the bump."

If you feel yourself getting hung up, a more pronounced bump is required: Twitch the rod downstream and at the same time perform a short strip. It's designed to dislodge a fly from its place on the bottom and send it upward a few inches as well as a few inches downstream. Your fly can and should drag and drift between bumps. That's what the bellied line accomplishes—it will pull the fly downstream just ahead of the boat and telegraph what's happening on the bottom with a tick, tick, tick. But the bump is necessary for the fish to recognize the fly as food. To put it short and sweet, vertical dredging is about getting your fly down to depth, putting a slight belly in it, staying tight to the fly as you drift along, and adding occasional bumps for action. And don't overthink the bump or manipulation of a dredging fly. The mechanics of bumping aren't all that different from the touch mend we discussed in chapter 4 for fishing Tequeelys grazingly over wood. Here we see precise, if subtle, line control again on display. We often tell anglers to just make an overexaggerated mend that will provide just the amount of movement necessary to remind the fish that what he's looking at is alive. But keep it to a minimum: Too much stripping, mending, or twitching will cause the fly to move up and out of the bottom twelve inches of the water column, which is—we repeat—*exactly* where we want it.

As far as hook sets go, we prefer a sharp, compact sweep to the side for this type of fishing. As we discussed before, smallmouth can swallow and expel food in the blink of an eye. If you detect a strike and set the hook with a big, vertical movement of the rod and the fish doesn't have the fly, your offering is now long gone. That fish is sitting down there wondering where his meal went to in such a hurry. By contrast, if you detect a strike and do a sharp set to the side (and don't lift all your line off the water) and the fish doesn't have the fly, you've only moved the fly a foot or two and the fish may still chase it down for a second chance. It's a given that any time you have to employ vertical dredging, things may be a little slow in terms of action. You simply can't afford to miss strikes and squander opportunities. Paying close attention to your line, staying in contact with the fly, and setting the hook properly will stack the odds in your favor.

Dredging is unquestionably the most difficult technique for anglers to master. There is a Zen-like sweet spot that comes from the angle of the cast, the mend, and the amount of tension you put on the fly. The bug needs to be sunk deep and dead-drifted a bit, but also bumped along periodically to provide motion and keep the fly from hanging up (it'll take some time, but eventually you'll learn to distinguish between a fish and a hang-up in the making). When fishing from a boat, the oarsman can control the drift speed and allow the angler to achieve the right angle and tension.

Perhaps no other technique requires as much savvy and precision from the boatsman as dredging. He or she must at once follow the contours of a deeper shelf while at the same time following the pace established by the tip of the fly line. If you hire a guide, odds are you can sit back, relax, and simply focus on your fishing. But if your fishing buddy is less of an expert on a given piece of water, do plenty of communicating. With dredging, everything must work together to keep the fly ticking along the bottom. If all the elements come together, dredging is a deadly technique. But if one of the elements goes haywire, getting into these lethargic, deepwater smallmouth can become quite, quite difficult.

Other Untapered Leader Situations: Fishing the Fall and Tight-Line Dredging

There are two more applications for fishing straight, untapered leaders—fishing the fall and tight-line dredging. Basically, fishing the fall means fishing vertical structure to which fish are holding tight. These might be wood seawalls, riprap banks, sheer rock faces, or other vertical structure. Conversely, tight-line dredging is basically a modification of the tight-line nymphing practiced in trout circles. The two approaches have fundamental differences, so we'll deal with them separately.

Smallmouth nets should have wide bottoms to cradle fish gently and naturally. HEIDI OBERSTADT

FISHING THE FALL

Fishing the fall takes advantage of bass's tendency to suspend just off vertical structure and gives us access to fish holding tight to structure but indifferent to surface flies. Fishing the fall uses a similar setup to vertical dredging, only without the indicator. When fishing the fall we aren't looking to suspend the fly; rather, we're trying to bump it down a vertical structure. Of course, you could deploy a tapered leader here as well, but using an untapered leader or hybrid leader (four and a half feet of tapered leader and four and a half feet of straight tippet) allows you to control drop speed and depth without necessarily going with a heavier fly. Using the weight of the fly to control speed of drop and depth when fishing the fall can be problematic, especially in calm or flat water. This is because fish are often holding within a foot or two of the surface, and splashing a heavy crayfish pattern down on their heads may spook as many fish as it seduces.

There's one other good reason to use untapered leaders when fishing the fall, and that's because a number of vertical structures tend to have conflicting currents—many times you will encounter a reverse current within the first foot or two of shore where the fish are holding. In these cases, it's often the situation that your fly line is moving downstream while your fly is moving up—and the drag created interferes with the fly's ability to drop. By going with an untapered leader, you are giving the current less of a material area to push or pull on.

The best fall-fishing flies are loosely imitative leech and crayfish patterns with material with plenty of passive action. Long strands of marabou, Flashabou, and schlappen and saddle hackle undulate compellingly on the drop. Just don't overdress these flies, since a sparser tie will allow the material to breathe more enticingly with minimal manipulation.

Before we talk about technique, let's look at occasions for fishing the drop. Straight vertical structure is pretty rare in natural riparian environments; straight vertical drops often come in the form of sheer rock faces. Even if the water drops down to extrememly deep water, bass will hang suspended just a few feet (or inches) below the surface, taking advantage of irregularities in the rock face to get out of current. Rivers with significant human development may possess even more vertical structure in the form of wood seawalls and riprap shoreline—both hold smallmouth bass. Up against a sharp rock wall or seawall, you can fish by feel. In the case of rock strucutre, fish hold tight and eat crayfish.

In these situations casts are often very, very short and need to be very precise. Essentially, all we're doing is letting the fly land and allowing it to fall either straight down under very gentle tension or walking down the bank like someone going down the stairs. With this type of fishing, the speed of the fall will be more important than the ultimate depth the fly achieves. So tie and select your flies with different sink rates in mind, the same way you might do while tying flies for cruising carp.

While the line and leader setup for fishing the fall may resemble vertical dredging, there are a number of differences. First, because we're not looking to suspend the fly at a given depth but letting it fall, we do away with the indicator. This gives us two options for detecting bites: watching the tip of the fly line and/or fishing by feel. Probably the best approach is to deploy both. You can do this by making sure you have both a tactile and visual connection to the fly the moment it hits the water and begins to fall. The visual connection part is easy—simply watch for your line to tick forward or to either side. The tactile connection is trickier, and it's most easily accomplished if, while the fly falls, you strip the line toward you in a very subtle, steady motion. Think of it less as a strip than as a tightening of your connection to the fly. Strike detection is a matter of feeling for anomalies to this sensation. Sometimes, an eat feels like nothing—in which case it's time to set the hook. Other times, it's a sudden feeling of heaviness in your fly—in which case it's time to set the hook.

Fishing the fall requires intense concentration to the slightest movements, but if done correctly it can work like magic when bass are moody and suspended near structure. KYLE ZEMPEL

When you do get bit on the fall, setting the hook with the rod instead of a strip set will give you multiple shots at a fish if you miss one—and missing smallmouth in this way is easy to do. As we've discussed elsewhere in the book, bass will often take pop crayfish (and crayfish imitations, which is what smallmouth understand a falling weighted fly to represent) in and out of their mouth several times in an attempt to find the right position for eating. In such cases where your set comes during one of these repositionings, a strip set will move the fly two to three feet, which may take it out of the bass's zone. A rod set, however, will move the fly far less. If you rod-set and miss the fish, quickly tighten up again and wait for the second strike. More often than not it will be imminent.

TIGHT-LINE DREDGING

The other unique occasion for untapered-leader fishing is tight-line dredging. This is really just a beefed-up version of tight-line nymphing as it's practiced in the trout world. It has a very singular application: when fishing in high cfs pocket water, usually the boulder fields in northern Minnesota, Wisconsin, and the Upper Peninsula of Michigan. While fly anglers typically don't have difficulty presenting within the topmost portion of this column, the lies big fish tend to prefer are in the deep water directly behind large boulders. It can be difficult for fly anglers to target those fish hanging directly behind boulders in faster water, simply because the drag on the fly line and leader makes it very difficult to get a fly to depth—again, a straight mono or fluoro connection works wonders here.

One advantage of pocket water and other seriously broken water is that you can often get right up next to the lie you're presenting to. The challenge involves getting down to depth, but the deeper gouges behind large boulders can hold good fish if you can get your fly down before the current whisks it out of the strike zone. NATE SIPPLE

To fish at depth directly behind these boulders in quick water requires not only as thin a straight leader as you can get away with, but also as heavy and as streamlined a fly. It's true that to get to depth we generally are making a compromise between the action of a fly and its ability to plummet—think heavy heads, slim, synthetic bodies, and ultrasparse tails with a touch of rubber and flash. You are not really casting these flies so much as lobbing them.

For these types of flies you might experiment with tying on undressed bass jigs from the conventional fishing department of your nearest big-box store. Or, if you are extra-entrepreneurial, you can smelt your own. Don't be afraid of big quarter-ounce, three-eights-ounce, and even half-ounce jigheads.

One other difference when fishing pocket water is usually how much closer you can get to the fish. Whether fishing on foot or from a boat, it's often possible to fish dredging flies with little to no fly line outside the tip of the rod—Czech nymphing, in other words. This tight-line connection to the fly will allow you to feel bites that might otherwise be difficult to detect in the roiling currents. Hook sets should be straight up. Fast action, five- and six-weight switch rods are fantastic for this technique, since they give excellent reach. The fly line you use makes no difference whatsoever, since it will stay in the rod for the entirety of the presentation. The only thing outside the rod is your untapered leader.

With lighter flies and tapered leaders, you may pick up the smaller fish from the pocket water, but by getting deeper with these dredging techniques, you'll be able to access pocket water buckets that are typically off-limits to fly anglers. While far from "pure" fly fishing, it can nonetheless be an effective tactic to experiment with, especially during summer when rafters, canoers, and kayakers drive fish into these relatively remote, safe lies.

CHAPTER 6

Other Voices: Essays and Interviews

Part I. Essays

Smallmouth habitat, geography, and geology vary widely across North America, and so does smallmouth behavior. In this final section of the book, we asked the best smallmouth minds of the modern era to speak at length about what makes their watersheds unique fisheries. In these pages you'll find tips on migratory fish, cold-water bassin', and the ingredients of the perfect popper. Incorporate these perspectives into your own evolving smallmouth fishing program and have worlds more success on the water.

While the ways to present to bass remain the same, bass behavior will differ by watershed, as the voices in this chapter can attest to. ERIC CHRISTENSEN

Big Water Smallmouth

Luke Kavajecz

Luke Kavajecz operates Freshcoast Angling, a Lake Superior guide service based out of Anglers All on the shores of Chequamegon Bay in Ashland, Wisconsin. Luke specializes in shallow water smallmouth bass fishing in Chequamegon Bay and nearshore brown trout fishing in the Apostle Islands. He lives in Ashland, Wisconsin.

Lake Superior is a big body of water that can be battered by gale-force winds, extremely cold temperatures, stormy waves, and thick pack ice. But within this inland sea is a fly-fishing paradise that presents a unique and challenging environment to target large smallmouth bass.

Although most of Lake Superior is much too cold and basically void of life, a few areas of the lake are perfectly suited for warm-water fish. One of these areas is Chequamegon Bay, a relatively warm and shallow offshoot of Lake Superior located along Wisconsin's South Shore. Sheltered by the Bayfield Peninsula and the Apostle Islands, the water in Chequamegon Bay is a haven for all fish that swim in Lake Superior, and it is a perfect habitat for smallmouth bass to grow and thrive in.

In order to successfully hunt along bright, sandy bottoms, the littoral bass of the Great Lakes are bright in color with marked striations. LUKE KAVAJECZ

Guide Luke Kavajecz at work on his home waters of Wisconsin's Chequamegon Bay. LUKE KAVAJECZ

The northern edges of the bay are bordered by steep sandstone cliffs and deep cold water, while the southern rim of the bay is shallow and sandy. The water warms enough to support a large forage base and, with it, smallmouth bass. This is not classic smallmouth habitat for the most part. Sandy bottom is the primary structure along with scattered wood. Rocks are hard to find.

Although the bay is relatively protected from the vast, open waters of Lake Superior, the big lake's effects are fully felt within the bay, and more than anything, the lake's winds, waves, and currents are what influence the mood of the smallmouth. Perhaps the biggest influence on the fish is the lake's wind-driven tidal movement, called a seiche. Much like water sloshes back and forth in a bathtub, the water within the lake is constantly moving in and out, ebbing and flowing like a hyperactive ocean tide that changes every forty-five minutes to an hour. Since many parts of the bay are shallow with a very gradual bottom contour, the full effects of the seiche are felt. The biggest misconception about fishing the open water of the Great Lakes versus fishing the water in a river is that the water on the lakes is flat and still. This couldn't be further from the truth. Just like the tide determines the way an angler would pursue saltwater fish on a flat, the seiche determines where smallmouth will be on the waters of Lake Superior's Chequamegon Bay. Like a river, the current influences how fish will relate to structure and how the fish will feed. Fish will move in and out of the current or locate themselves along a current break to put themselves in the perfect spot to ambush baitfish. Seiche tidal movements are probably the single biggest influence on the mood of big-water smallmouth like those found in Lake Superior and in the shallow water areas of northern Lake Michigan.

As soon as the ice is gone from the bay, which can be as early as mid-April or as late as mid-May, the smallmouth begin to move into shallow flats adjacent to deep channels. Open-water smallmouth are creatures of "the edge," meaning when there isn't much cover, the fish will relate to a break or contour on a flat. This break can be as little as a one-foot drop in depth or as much as a twenty-foot drop in depth. Areas within the bay's sand flats that have these defined edges as well as cover on top of the flat are prime sites to find fish throughout the early season. Many smallmouth will stay shallow all year long, but a large portion of the population will migrate toward deeper water and offshore structure after the spawn in pursuit of baitfish. Generally, the "schoolie"-size smallmouth in the twelve- to sixteen-inch range remain shallow, while the big fish move offshore. The summer months are prime time to search out and actively look for feeding fish that break off from the deeper schooling fish and move shallow throughout the day. While the water is still calm in the early morning during summer, it's best to approach the flats quietly and slowly. Fish will show themselves, usually in the form of crashing baitfish. Birds are another indicator of where fish may be, and the common tern, which nests on the bay, is a great bird to follow.

Both bass and birds are in pursuit of the emerald shiner, which, along with young smelt and stickleback minnows, is the main forage base of the bay's smallmouth. Unlike many other smallmouth fisheries, which rely heavily on crayfish, there isn't a large population within the bay and the fish don't rely on the crayfish as a main source of food. In general, small baitfish patterns that imitate these types of forage are the best flies day in and day out, although these big, open-water fish will actively take topwater flies as well. Low-light periods, such as early morning and evening, as well as days with cloud cover and calm winds and waves, are the best topwater conditions. I've found that longer, narrow topwater flies that look more like baitfish than terrestrials or the classic bass popper seem to work better at fooling these fish on top. Like a river, the fish will also key in on insect hatches in the open water. The hexagenia mayfly hatch is massive on the bay, and the fish will gorge themselves on this big bug. Large caddis also hatch later in the summer, and this will present some awesome surface fishing if the conditions come together. By late September, the majority of Great Lakes smallmouth, including those in Chequamegon Bay, transition to deeper water and begin to school and feed heavily at the onset of cooler weather and the approaching winter. This transition usually signals the end of the pursuit of these fish on a fly.

The Great Lakes are an awesome place to pursue fish on a fly. The smallmouth bass that grow in these waters are some of the biggest to be found and are a great resource for fly anglers looking for a unique Midwestern fly-fishing experience.

Migratory Fish of the Great Lakes Tributaries

Nate Sipple

In the spring of the year, anglers on certain watersheds can find another aspect of smallmouth migration. This is the migration of smallmouth bass up into smaller rivers from larger bodies of water. In the Great Lakes region, there exists some of the largest smallmouth bass in the world. Most of the year these fish have all they need and more out in the vast expanses of water that they call home. Finding smallmouth in these massive bodies of water can be a bit like finding a needle in a haystack. However, as winter loosens her icy grip on the Great Lakes and nearshore temps start to rise, some smallmouth will opt to fulfill their spawning rituals in the tributaries that flow into these lakes. It's during this time that anglers have a legitimate shot at smallmouth that can tip the scales at six pounds or more. Like most fish that run into rivers to spawn, smallmouth will enter these rivers sometimes weeks before they actually spawn. This pre-spawn phase offers anglers amazing opportunities at trophy smallmouth that they might otherwise never encounter. Many of the same techniques that work late in the year will again work early in the year. Low and slow is the name of the game. Many of these fish have gone through months of wintering, with very little in the way of active feeding occurring.

As spring approaches and the females are growing eggs, their metabolic rate increases and the desire to feed before the spawn is amplified. Weight that was lost over the winter months needs to be replaced before searching for an area to spawn. Since these fish are not "locals" to these rivers, finding them with any consistency can be challenging. You can narrow your search significantly by being able to recognize the type of water that smallmouth prefer this time of the year. Areas with little to no current and a dark bottom are a good bet. These areas warm quickly and often contain baitfish. Basically, the smallmouth want to work as little as possible, while still being able to feed regularly. Depending on the depth of the river, your best bet will likely be an intermediate or sink tip line. A short fluorocarbon tippet section with a baitfish pattern or leech pattern is a great choice. Give each spot a fair amount of time before moving on, as the fish can be lazy and need to see the fly several times before committing. Remember, smallmouth are not built like trout or salmon. They're not likely to migrate many miles up shallow, fast water and through heavy rapids. The bottom couple miles of most tributaries seem to hold the majority of these migratory smallmouth, so work those areas first.

Nate Sipple rows Tim Landwehr through some wide river as it approaches the mouth of a big-water bay. HEIDI OBERSTADT

Spring is an exciting time on these tributaries for fly anglers. With basically one line and one fly, anglers can have a legit shot at migratory trout that are falling back to the lake, walleye, pike, and monstrous smallmouth. Be flexible and willing to vary your retrieve (pace) until you find what the fish are in the mood for. Just because the fish are acting lethargic doesn't mean that they won't eat a big fly, either. I've actually had success switching to a much larger fly after watching fish follow time and time again. It's possible that they see it as a more significant intake of calories, for the same amount of work. If you want to catch the biggest smallmouth of your life on a fly, plan a trip to the Great Lakes tributaries in the spring. It is a small window, but a six-pound-plus smallmouth will make you thankful you tried.

Understanding Fishing "the Crash"

Kyle Zempel

Kyle Zempel currently resides in the rural bluffs of Black Earth, Wisconsin, where in 2013, he created Black Earth Angling Co. (www.blackearthangling.com), a fly-fishing guide outfit focused on providing clients with one-of-a-kind fishing experiences. Kyle guides for the trout of the Driftless area and the diverse warm-water opportunities of the Wisconsin River. He's become well known for his guide work on the Wisconsin River, specifically in fishing "the crash," as well as his work with a camera in the field as a fly-fishing photographer.

The southern sections of the Wisconsin River, known as the Lower Wisconsin River (LWR), make up a vast, ever-changing body of water that greatly differs from the northern sections. The LWR is the longest free-flowing section of river in the entire Midwest and cuts through the heart of the "Driftless" region. The LWR is wide (1,500 feet in some spots) and shallow, with the river floor primarily made up of sand and limestone. Unlike the rocky-bottomed northern sections that remain relatively unchanged, the sandy bottoms of the LWR cause the "channels" to shift daily. Fallen timber, sudden drop-offs, and islands make up the majority of the key structure. Needless to say, the LWR is not your classic smallmouth water and often requires the angler to stray from the classic fishing techniques to find success.

The LWR has one of the best schooling baitfish (emerald shiner and shad) populations in the state. Due to the amount of sand, the crawfish are not as abundant as one would find in the northern sections, thus baitfish are the main food source for the LWR smallmouth bass. As the water warms and the bass finish their spring spawn, you will begin to find mobs of smallmouth

When not dining on cork, guide Kyle Zempel is a big-river smallmouth specialist. KYLE ZEMPEL

pushing schools of baitfish on shallow flats and around structure. This phenomenon will start to occur in late May and can last through September; however, the peak occurs in June and July. I have deemed this phenomenon "the crash," and it is often compared to the striper bait blitz out East. This is what makes the LWR smallmouth unique.

To properly fish the crash, you must first understand what it is you're after. The most common mistake I run into is an angler trying to find the smallmouth. In a changing river where your targeted species feeds on bait, you must find the bait before you find your target species. Find the bait, find the bass. Schooling bait often travel throughout the river system, and where you find bait one day, you may not find them the next. This is a key piece of information that an angler must understand in order to find success on a body of water like the LWR.

THE OASIS THEORY

A big sandy river can be looked at like a desert. Sand does not provide safe cover, thus in theory one can write off a large majority of the vast, shallow sand flats. In a desert, an oasis is an area that draws life. The LWR has these similar oasis areas, which draw life and attract the bait. Where you find the bait, you will find the bass (and many other species of game fish). The oasis area can vary in size and complexity but is often an area of greater than the average depth for that section of river. Once an oasis area is identified, an angler must begin breaking down the area into sub-oasis areas (fallen timber, islands, troughs, flooded vegetation, current breaks) and work over these areas thoroughly, keeping a watchful eye for skittering bait.

So how does one go about finding the bait? Treat each day as its own. As mentioned, the LWR changes week to week, month to month, and year to year. I often see anglers go to the same spots repeatedly and find spotty success. The angler will go to a spot where they had success, which to the average angler appears unchanged from their previous outing; the same fallen tree, same depth, but no bass. The angler is puzzled. Why are the bass not here? Is it the wrong lure/fly? Is it the weather? What the angler fails to realize is that he is in the oasis area but not in the correct sub-oasis area. Today the bait are not seeking shelter in the angler's spot, and it is not the lure/fly or the weather that is the reason for the bass not feeding. The bass *are* feeding, but only where there is food (aka bait). Anglers must remain mobile and willing

When fishing "the crash," both bass and bass angler can get their fill. And then some. KYLE ZEMPEL

to search nearby areas until they find the bait. Generally, the bait won't move far. Look to the next nearest structure in the oasis and start there. Find the bait, find the bass.

HOW TO CATCH CRASHING BASS

Crashing bass will get your heart pumping, and I have witnessed some of the best casters fall apart while fishing the crash. The mobs of bass will corral/herd the schools of bait, which often forces the bait to break the surface. What follows is a lot of explosive chomping and splashing while the bass gorge on the helpless bait. This crashing often will come in waves. The bass crash the bait and retreat, allowing the bait to re-school, and then the process will repeat itself. The duration between crashes can vary greatly depending on the time of year and amount of bait in the oasis. During the peak, crashing can occur every minute. Allowing time for the bait to re-school is key, and overcasting will delay this process.

The trick to hooking these crashing bass is to time your casting with the waves of attacking fish and then quickly retrieve, readying yourself for the next attack. The baitfish are skipping/raining out of the water, running for their lives. The smallmouth are keyed into this movement. A baitfish popper pattern that skips on the surface is ideal when fishing to crashing bass. Unlike popper fishing in the northern regions where you often dead-drift or slowly retrieve your popper, the LWR bass expect your popper to move with haste. Remember, we are trying to imitate the fleeing baitfish. Your retrieve should be fast, short, and choppy with a pause or two mixed in. The speed often gathers the attention of numerous bass, and the angler should be ready for multiple bass to attempt striking on the pause. If there are numerous anglers fishing, the partner without the hooked fish should cast behind the partner's hooked fish for an easy double hookup.

Smallmouth Outside the "Box"

Bart Landwehr

What do successful people, regardless of where they have found success, invariably seem to have in common? I believe it to be an almost innate willingness to challenge the status quo, and in doing so, they oftentimes shift ideas about how things can be done. Whether in business, politics, activism, music, art, or in this case fishing, thinking differently can open a whole new set of doors. When I started fly fishing for smallmouth bass, it was standard practice to "dredge" minnow and crayfish patterns during the heat of the day, and if you were lucky, a "popper bite" might present itself in the early morning or late afternoon over still, glassy waters. We caught fish, and some were big, but the whole practice was quick to become mundane . . . enter the Murdich Minnow.

Bart Landwehr prepares to deliver a damselfly pattern to the head of a long riffle. During the warm, buggy days of summer when there's no shortage of food throughout the water column, smallmouth fishing can be pleasantly technical. NATE SIPPLE

Learning your favorite smallmouth river by boat and by foot will gain you the greatest understanding of it. HEIDI OBERSTADT

Upon first glance, the oversized saltwater streamer that has since effectively revolutionized a whole new breed of smallmouth fly was so flamboyantly different from the usual suspects that it almost didn't seem right. It was Las Vegas, and we were used to Clintonville. That all changed on a hot June afternoon many seasons ago while I was guiding a gentleman on what I would consider an average day. We were fishing some off-bank drops with crayfish patterns and finding just enough action to keep us interested. At the time I had a couple of Murdichs in a dark corner of the streamer box, and after losing a fly to the river (as can be common with a weighted fly and a gnarly bottom), my eye caught the aforementioned streamer as I went in for a retie. What the hell? Right? My client was very interested in casting anything lighter than the anvil he had been heaving all day, and this "why not?" decision in fly selection effectively changed my whole approach to smallmouth fly fishing.

What we saw for the next couple of hours was as close to fishing nirvana as I've ever been. Bass, and big ones at that, uncorked themselves in desperate attempts at raining down hellfire on that flashy crippled minnow. The fly set down with no huge disturbance, and, rather than drop like a stone, it hovered in a neutral zone, where it kicked and quivered in death throes like a minnow on its last go-round. The bass couldn't pass up such an easy meal. A concept so basic, yet so profoundly outside my thinking at that point, broke down a lot of barriers in fishing techniques. No longer was I tied to the "what works" mentality; instead, I now possessed the "what if" approach to looking at my favorite waters.

Heading into my fifteenth year of guiding smallmouth, I consider myself less sure of a black-and-white path to fish and instead have learned to take each day as a singular event, trying to use my time on the water to understand its pulse. Many great anglers I have fished with over the years seem to find ways to catch a fish when few others can. What they do and how they think can be a mystery if you don't loosen up the possibilities a bit. It seems that when you forget to "know" how to catch smallmouth, and instead pay more attention to how they are reacting to their day, an average outing can become extraordinary.

I have learned too that sometimes a big bass will happily slurp a beetle or dead-drifted hopper, only if fed perfectly down and across, and will spook explosively from a popper or your best baitfish pattern. I have seen bass switch feeding areas multiple times throughout a very consistent weather day, as well as bug preference. Look at a good spot, I mean really look at it, and oftentimes you will begin to see. This is definitely an exercise in patience, as truly watching to learn a given spot's ins and outs is often done best without making a cast.

In the end, there are myriad tactics available to the interested smallmouth angler, and most of them hold some honest to goodness validity; that being said, each method has its place and won't necessarily work on each outing. Be on the water as much as possible, and try to approach fishing as the great enigma it sometimes seems to be. Let the fish show you what they want, and how they want it, then smile like an idiot once you figure them out . . . I still do every time.

The Small-Fly Phenomenon

Tim Landwehr

I have had the good fortune to have been a smallmouth bass guide for the majority of my adult life. During this period, it has been so much fun to watch how the sport has changed and developed. In the beginning it simply was an extension of what we already had learned in the trout fishing game. We adapted our techniques from the trout world and forced a square peg into a round hole, and this worked with just enough success to continue down the same path for far too long. The Woolly Bugger remained a constant in our arsenal for years, and large gaudy poppers would be our answer when "the water was warm enough for a topwater bite." While nymphing techniques, gaudy poppers, and the good old Woolly Buggers still have a place in the sport, so much has been learned.

Our staff of guides have watched fly patterns progress and change quickly with so many more anglers flocking to chase smallmouth. More anglers pursuing these fish pushes the limits on fly design and what really works on a consistent basis. Looking at the direction smallmouth fishing has gone in the last five years, I have seen a huge push to rattles, articulated bodies, and overall giant flies. The smallmouth is an opportunistic predator, so it seems to just make sense. When you look at the conventional side of angling, you see anglers throwing giant soft plastics, explosive walk-the-dog topwater baits and whatever else can push ten gallons of water. They do this because it can grab the attention of a fish that is in the aggressive feeding mode or the player. We have now watched many fly anglers virtually put all of their eggs in the big-fly basket and feel that this is how you catch trophy smallmouth.

We as fly fishermen can learn an enormous amount from the gear anglers in this sport. That is how the big-fly technique evolved from the lonely Woolly Bugger. Big flies, big fish seems to be the overall theory. With that said, I noticed a shift a few years back when numbers of gear guys started to trickle into my shop looking for very specific tying materials. They would mill around the shop, not ask for help, make their purchases, and hastily exit. They were afraid I was going to find out about a secret that was held closely at that time by only a few of the top anglers. You see, each year a huge bass tournament takes place in Door County, Wisconsin, with some of the most elite conventional circuit fishermen competing. The elite pros were the guys shopping at my store. It turned out to be so silly I just couldn't believe it. They had been tying very small and crudely constructed marabou jigs in natural colors and winning it all. Now the secret is out and it is commonplace, but these tiny jigs had been outfishing most of the garlic-and-salt chemistry experiment baits

Nate Sipple prepares to make a delicate cast to a sighted fish. HEIDI OBERSTADT

on the market. The anglers explained to me how the fish would move slowly along the flats and simply "pick 'em up." The bigger stuff was spooking the larger fish off the shelves, and they would not attack. Finesse smallmouth fishing with gear was outfishing everything else, even for the trophy bass.

A number of years back, I had the distinct pleasure to get to fish with a man by the name of Jack Allen. Jack is a largemouth bass guide in Florida and is truly one of the most interesting and unique men I have ever met. Jack was to fish with us for eight days, and I have never met a man with such a passion for popping for bass. Jack's favorite rod sizes for smallmouth were four- and five-weight rods loaded with eight- or even nine-weight lines! These rods were far too small for the size of flies we had been casting or for that matter the power and size of the fish that swim in our river. The overlining of the rod was something I still can't seem to wrap my head around, but Jack could handle the setup masterfully.

We began our day and I tied on a Murdich Minnow, which has become a staple fly for our guide staff. After about ten minutes Jack politely asked me to "please take this horrible giant fly off." I agreed of course and moved into my topwater box and tied on a Boogle Bug. I will say in my defense that the Boogle Bug is not a big popper by any stretch of the imagination. This fly however still was not Jack's cup of tea, and he asked if we could possibly use something he brought along. He looked me square in the eye and quoted

Small-fly aficionado Jack Allen shows off one of his favorite high-vis bass bugs. NATE SIPPLE

James A. Henshall—"don't forget the spiders." He pulled out a fly box that had a masking-tape label that read Neuvo Spidaire on it in black Magic Marker. It was a simple rubber-legged, sponge-bodied spider that looked much more like a bluegill fly than a topwater smallie bug.

We fished over rock-bottom flats that ranged in depth from twelve inches to two feet. What I saw next would change me forever. I watched an eighteen-inch fish swim slowly over to the fly and sip it in exactly like a cutthroat. We fished similar water for the next eight days with the same result over and over again. Over the years we began to experiment with larger poppers in the same areas and what we found was that sometimes the big pop of or even the overall size of the bug would not interest or might even frighten the fish. I have fished grassy banks with clients with big streamers and poppers and taken a fish or two off of what should be the most prime water we have. I will do a row up and fish some of these smaller low-profile patterns over the exact water we just fished and take three or four with the exact same slow cutthroat rise. The long and short of it is it really works and has truly added to customers' overall experience on the water.

When we look at smallmouth bass in the river, we have players and then we have fish that can be coaxed into eating if the opportunity is easy. Throwing big flies and covering huge amounts of water is absolutely a perfect method when you're truly looking for players, and I fully understand that part of the game. I, however, have come to enjoy fooling more technical fish, fish that hold in weed lines, or fish that drift quietly out of a shadow or stalk a fly for a long distance while my customer and I watch the entire thing unfold in front of us. Fishing small bugs has become such a strong part of our guides' game that we have categorized these flies as Wigglies. They are basically small low-profile patterns that are fairly similar to the Chernobyl ant or a Fat Albert. Whatever it is, the smallmouth eat them slowly and with absolute confidence—they seem to know that it's a meal that can't escape.

Do I think Wigglies is the only way to fish smallmouth with small flies? Absolutely not, but it has truly changed how I approach so many spots on the river. This technique is responsible for my catching many fish that I know would not have eaten a big bug in the water they were holding in. I think this just adds to the overall continued knowledge of fishing smallmouth with the fly. We are pushing the limits with new materials, fly design, and talented anglers that can think outside the box. But one of those boxes we might find ourselves stuck in is our obsession with big flies. If we have set rules to what works and what doesn't, we just stand still and never grow. If you're a tier, remember that innovation also happens at the other end of the fly-size spectrum: with small flies.

Smallmouth Flies, Then and Now

Tom Andersen

Tom Andersen retired from the fly-fishing business after working for twenty-two years as a manufacturer's rep for Umpqua Feather Merchants, Sage, Simms, and RIO. He also served as a guide for many years in northern Wisconsin. He currently hunts and fishes out of his home base in River Falls, Wisconsin.

Growing up in northwest Wisconsin, my introduction to fly fishing was fishing for panfish and smallmouth bass. My tools were pretty basic. I started with a tubular aluminum fly rod and a South Bend Oren-O-Matic fly reel with who knows what kind of fly line. My first smallmouth on the fly came on a Prescott Spinner Fly, and the fly was a large Yellow Sally.

Later, in the early 1960s, I guided anglers for a lodge on a well-know smallmouth river near where I lived. I was in awe of my "sport's" UMCO Possum Belly tackle box loaded with what were then state-of-the-art flies for smallmouth. Cal-Mac Bugs, Wilder-Dilg Sliders, Feath-Orenos, and Peck's Poppers filled those trays. I'd never seen so many flies for smallmouth. I was hooked. A lifelong love affair with flies for bronzebacks had begun.

Tom Andersen hoists a fine early summer fish that ate a leech pattern. TOM ANDERSEN

Having sold flies in a retail setting and worked as the representative for Umpqua Feather Merchants, I've seen many changes in smallmouth flies over the past forty years. But some things haven't changed. Most anglers who pursue smallmouth with the fly still prefer to take them on top! Credit E. H. Peckinpaugh (Peck's Poppers), Will Dilg, and E. B. Wilder (Wilder-Dilg Slider) for sure. They were the early 1900s pioneers developing topwater cork and flies. Today, multicolored rubber legs, flash material, and marabou festoon the more modern versions. Flies like Umpqua Feather Merchants' new bass poppers featuring high-quality hooks, and special designs are crafted specifically for smallmouth bass.

While deer-hair bass bugs have taken a backseat to the easy-to-fish cork and foam bugs, they still play an important role. I would certainly credit Orley Tuttle's Devil Bug (1920s) with launching us on a deer-hair bass bug journey, and the Messinger Frog (1930s) is still a featured fly with Umpqua to this day. Dave Whitlock's classic deer-hair bugs continue to account for many caught bass. Larry Dahlberg's Diving Minnow, Diving Bug, Rabbit Strip Diver, and deer-hair Dilg-Slider really moved us beyond the traditional deer-hair bug in the 1980s and 1990s. Flashabou and dumbbell lead eyes, however, were real game changers.

Larry once proclaimed that the Dahlberg Diver was an underwater delivery system for Flashabou. That pretty well sums up just how important the advent of Flashabou was, and how it opened the floodgates for flash materials. Around the same time period, Tom Schmuecker of Wapsi Fly, Inc., came up with small lead dumbbell eyes as a way to get flies deeper. And then, Bob Clouser, using those eyes, created the historic Clouser Swimming Minnow, which really changed the landscape.

More recent fly innovations for smallmouth have often mimicked the success of conventional tackle favorites like the Lazy Ike (Wiggle Minnow), the Zara Spook (Spook-R & Pole Dancers), the Jitterbug (Schmidterbug), sinking Rapala (Gummy Minnows), and of course lead head jigs (Meat Whistles), to name a few. Smallmouth bass aren't fussy. They just like to chow down. It gives fly tiers and designers great latitude. That said, a smallmouth bass might just swim up to your popper, nose it out of the water, and then swim away without eating it. The next fish might take the popper out of the air before it even hits the water.

For the foreseeable future I think we'll continue to see old reliable flies reinvented, more good subsurface patterns, some cool new swimming flies, some great crossover patterns being applied to the sport (think Tequeely), and, maybe with a bit of luck, some more fun topwater bugs!

Big Flies

Kip Vieth

Kip is a Minnesota-based Orvis-endorsed guide and 2015 Guide of the Year nominee. He has more than thirty years of experience and is the host and outfitter for the Orvis Musky Schools. Kip is a popular speaker and writer for numerous fishing shows, clubs, and publications. He currently lives in Monticello, Minnesota, where he owns and operates Wildwood Float Trips (wildwoodfloattrips.com).

I'm fortunate enough to live on the banks of what I feel is the greatest warmwater fly-fishing river in the country, the Upper Mississippi River. Now I know that I'm a bit biased, but its wide variety of trophy species, such as smallmouth bass, muskies, walleye, northern pike, and carp, make it truly a unique and wonderful piece of water. The state of Minnesota has also placed very aggressive catch-and-release regulations on it to ensure that it will be that way for generations to come. When one mentions the Mississippi River, it often conjures up visions of Mark Twain's books and the big, wide, muddy river on which Tom Sawyer and Huck Finn's adventures took place. Nothing could be further from the truth. Here in Minnesota the river often looks like

Kip Vieth shows off a great Minnesota smallmouth that crushed an oversized streamer. JON LUKE

a Western trout river. It can be as clear as any spring creek and often just as temperamental. It is still a large river and it takes some time to learn its moods and character, but once the puzzle pieces start falling together its bounty is revealed to the patient angler and all is right in the world.

One of the biggest and often most daunting pieces to the puzzle is high water. In the early part of the season, spring thaw and showers can turn that peaceful spring creek from last August into a torrid beast. One also has to keep in mind that the Mississippi basin is vast. A large rain event 150 miles upstream can affect the river when you least expect it. Anglers often look at the river when these events happen and often just say forget it. When the river goes from 3,000 cfs to 10,000 cfs in a day or two, it can seem as if the river is doomed until it settles back down. That is not always the case. The angler has to stay in the game and try to get the puzzle piece to fit. Most fly anglers don't know that it can be one of the most productive times of the year for truly world-class river smallmouth.

You have been tying flies all week in preparation for your day on the river. You were so excited that you forgot to look at the river gauge. When you arrive at the landing, you see that the river has come up two feet since the last time you were here. Your heart sinks, and if you were most people you'd curse a little and probably leave and go to a plan-B piece of water. How are

Smallmouth can make unpredictable moves at any stage of the fight. Be ready to made sudden changes with the rod to accommodate aerial acrobatics. HEIDI OBERSTADT

In crystal-clear lake environments, fly size should correlate to the size of available prey items. Save your biggest, shock-and-awe style streamers for river fishing. LUKE KAVAJECZ

you ever going to learn to fish higher water unless you tough it out? I have had numerous clients quit on me only because the water was high and dirty. Once a quitting client's partner kept plugging away, and sure enough he pulled one of the largest smallmouth of the year out right from under the quitter's nose. A valuable lesson was learned.

When the water gets high and dirty, you really need to look at the situation as a fish sees it. All of a sudden their world has been turned upside down. They're just looking for a place to weather out the storm just as everything else in the river is. To the angler this means any quiet area. I kind of look at these spots like highway rest areas. They are usually off the main highway but still close enough to see what is going by. You also have to remember that most of the bait is looking for a place to hide also. Most everything in the river is forced into these rest areas. The smallmouth will be waiting. The fish have to eat, and the concentration of both predator and prey into these spots can make for some very productive days. Look to eddies, quiet areas behind islands and points, and don't forget those logjams and sweepers. These become my go-to areas when the conditions call for them.

When the water is up and dark, the fish need to either see, feel, or hear what they are after. In my fly selection for these conditions, I try to cover two if not all three of those criteria. My high-water flies are pretty basic. I try to stay away from crayfish patterns because they are hard to fish in high-water situations and I don't find them very effective. Ninety percent of the flies I am throwing are large flashy minnow patterns or large cork poppers. When I look for a good minnow pattern, I often think of my musky flies. They need to push a lot of water underneath the surface and have a ton of flash that helps to trigger a strike and makes them easier to see.

I will often tie a magnum Murdich Minnow, which is about 50 percent larger than your normal commercially tied version. In that pattern I add more flash, will sometimes add a rattle, and build a larger head so that it pushes more water underneath the surface as it is stripped. This fly can't help but get noticed. I will also take my 3M minnow and bulk it up to have a similar effect. Both these patterns are my go-to subsurface patterns when the water is up. I fish these patterns pretty slow. Strip them and give them a long pause so the fish can hunt them down. It is often hard to do with the swift currents, so mending can often be your best friend. You can also shorten your leader so you can have better control over your fly in these situations.

Most people don't think of high water as a good time to throw topwater presentations. Nothing could be further from the truth. Often the smallmouth are glued to the bank to give themselves some protection from the current. If a big popper hits them on the head, most times they simply can't resist it. When I say big, I mean big. One of my guides started fishing big cork poppers one spring with great success. They're the simplest of flies, and they're not pretty, but they show up for work and get the job done. I call them the Blue Collar Poppers. They are simply the old test tube cork stoppers that you can remember from your school days. Simply cut a groove in them and epoxy a hook in them. Paint to the color of your choice. Tie in a bunch of flash. Then tie in either marabou or artic fox hair for a tail. (I prefer arctic fox—it holds up a bit better.) Tie in some hackle for a collar and you're good to go. Most of our poppers are three-quarters of an inch to one and a quarter inches across the face. They move a ton of water and give a great sound that seems to really get the smallmouth's attention. They are very tough and last forever. Topwater fishing is always fun, but when the high water pushes every smallmouth in town to the bank, it can be epic.

High water can often be a real challenge. Unless you would rather stay home and mow the lawn, don't let it deter you from fishing. Think of the puzzle, and this is just another piece you need to figure out to be a truly successful angler. That is why I love guiding so much. There is always another piece to figure out. I know that the puzzle will never be complete, but finding that piece that was hiding in plain view and putting it together is where the real sense of accomplishment comes from.

"Making It Your Own"

Austin Adduci

Captain Austin Adduci currently resides in Orland Park, Illinois, a suburb of Chicago. He founded Grab Your Fly Charters in 2009 and was the original fly-fishing guide in the Chicagoland area. He guides multiple bodies of water for smallmouth, including Lake Michigan, Beaver Island, and all of Chicago's local rivers. He is an innovative tier and has smallmouth patterns in production with Catch Fly Fishing. He has been mentioned in Eastern Fly Fishing *magazine, Jerry Darkes's book* Fly Fishing the Inland Oceans, *and has been on many local TV shows. He can be found online at www.grabyourflycharters.com.*

The modern angler has a lot of information to negotiate, whether it's the hot fly on Facebook or an article in a magazine or a whole book on a single species, like this one. But to take full advantage of all the information available, you've also got to remember to avoid the one major pitfall that too many modern anglers fall subject to: getting lazy.

They don't know they're lazy, of course, and they aren't lazy in terms of the physical work of fishing. They're casting hard, stripping hard, all that good

Captain Austin Adduci puts the muscle to a big Beaver Island smallmouth bass. DAVE KARCZYNSKI

On any given day or river, bass behavior may or may not conform to precedence or your expectations. Being flexible and staying open-minded is as important for everyday anglers as it is for full-time guides. DAVE HOSLER

stuff. The laziness is a mental one. It comes from not thinking enough about what they're doing, from outsourcing too much of their decision making to things other people are doing. They sit at work, they see stuff on the Internet, and they think, "Hey, I'll just go and do that on my river this weekend." And that's the wrong approach. Just because you saw a huge bass on Facebook with x fly in its mouth in x part of the country doesn't necessarily mean that fly is going to work in your region on your water on a given day. So when it comes time to actually start fishing, use all the expert info you encounter as a starting point, but remember that you've got to make it your own in order to be as successful as you can be.

A lot of my clientele in the Chicagoland area fish widely. They're in Minnesota and Wisconsin and Pennsylvania and the Upper Peninsula of Michigan. And they often try to bring their same techniques to my river, which isn't always the best idea. The river I fish in Illinois is big and wide, averaging 150 yards in width with an average depth of three feet. It can get muddy in a hurry—as in six inches of visibility muddy. Fish are right against the banks. And I'll have clients throw a popper and not move it. And of course that's because they were on a river in another party of the Midwest a few weeks ago and, on that river, dead-drifted bugs are the way to go. On my river, however, they aren't.

I'll ask these guys, "What are you doing?"

"We don't move these things," they'll say.

To which I'll respond: "Here we move it. And don't just move it. Pop it hard. And keep it going all the way back to the boat."

These anglers are generally resistant until popping all the way back to the boat starts to work. That's because in the high, dirty water I often guide in, you need to give the fish a sound to follow. Yes, a smallmouth might initially see that fly land, but then with six inches of visibility they're suddenly thinking, "Where did that bug go?" They don't see it anymore. And so you need to give them a trail to follow, make some noise. It doesn't work on all rivers. But it's the only way to roll on mine. And the only way to know what your river is like is not to get pigeonholed by what others are doing, or even by what you yourself were doing the year before. Rivers change and fish assume different tendencies, and the only way to stay on top of the game is to watch what's going on right in front of you and adapt to it.

And that's what the most successful anglers do: adapt. They aren't just copycatting. They're taking somebody else's idea, tweaking it, twisting it, whatever, and making it work for themselves on their home waters. This modern age of information is a good thing because it lets people share and you see what everybody else is doing. And books like this one are incredible sources of information. But the next step, the most important one after you've finished an article or even a whole book like this one, is to grab your fly and your rod and go out there and make your fishing your own.

Part II. Interviews

Interview: Chuck Kraft on Sharp Silhouettes and the Benefits of Floating Lines

Chuck Kraft has well over thirty years of guiding under his belt and still guides part-time. Chuck has been tying flies since 1959, and his original patterns like the CK Nymph and Brer Rabbit were built using natural materials. In the very early 1990s, some of Chuck's clients who were in the furniture industry brought him a milk crate of fabric materials to use for tying flies. From that point on, Chuck's fly designs took a leap into the future of fly tying. Chuck based some of his fly designs after successful baits used by conventional fisherman, like the "Super Fluke" (CK Baitfish), the "Pig-N-Jig" (Clawdad), and the Panther Martin Spinner (Kreelex). Chuck's designs have won fly-fishing tournaments across the country and are amazing crossover patterns that fish just as well if not better in salt water. Chuck still ties flies professionally for Eastern Trophies Fly Fishing, along with other shops in Virginia. Chuck currently lives in Charlottesville, Virginia, with his wife, Shirley. Chuck's fly patterns, tails, fly-tying kits, and materials can be found at Eastern Trophies Fly Fishing (easterntrophies.com).

DK: What rivers were your flies designed on?

CK: The three main rivers I was guiding during the development of my flies were the James, the Shenandoah, and the New. The New is one of the oldest rivers in the world. And the Shenandoah is a miniature version of the New. As far as the New goes, I've done a lot of fishing in the tailwaters below Claytor Lake down to the West Virginia line. There's some really deep holes in there that I think Lefty talked to you about.

DK: Talk to us about the development of your flies. They are pretty unique designs.

CK: Sure. First off, all the research and design for these flies took place back in the 1990s. I was guiding for a living and so I had to produce fish for folks. We were getting a lot of refusals on the bugs we were fishing, and so I started working on designs to solve the problem of how to convert finicky bass. We fish a lot of low, clear water down there, so the more realistic detail you can put into those flies, the better.

One thing I started to notice about a lot of the flies we were fishing is that there were a lot of opportunities for them to lose their shape. They might get knocked around in the current or get fouled. Or sometimes the

Guide and fly-designer Chuck Kraft works one of his baitfish patterns through a hole on a Virginia tailwater. CHUCK KRAFT

materials would flatten and compress at a pivotal moment when a fish was right underneath the bug. I wanted flies that kept their shape no matter what. With some of the natural minnow patterns, you stop them and they lose their profile. And I noticed fish veering away from these flies at the last second.

So I started to experiment with different tailing material—trying to move away from feathers and such. I started with animal skins—I took sheep skin and rabbit skin and shaved the hair from the hide and used that to cut claws and tails. If you look at my flies, all of them have a real sharp silhouette. That is very much by design.

The silhouette of course was only part of it. Then there was all the work getting the flies to swim like they were supposed to. It was a pretty involved process.

DK: I notice that your current flies don't use animal skin. When did you make the switch to synthetic tail and claw material?

CK: In 1994 a furniture designer brought me a grocery bag full of a product called ultrasuede. It had a major advantage over animal skin because it wouldn't dry out and harden like animal skin would.

DK: And did the fish like it as well?

CK: Did they! We always did pretty well, but after the sharp silhouettes we were suddenly catching fish like nobody else. It was shocking the difference these materials made.

We did so well I kept my flies a secret for a good long while. I didn't reveal any of the flies or the patterns to the public until 2005—and by that time I had been fishing them for over a decade. It wasn't easy keeping things under wraps. I almost had to strip-search my clients after a day of fishing to get my flies back.

DK: What's a key to fishing some of these patterns correctly?

CK: The first thing you need to look at is what you're trying to imitate and learn to make your flies move like that. A lot of people have never seen a crawfish swim, they just jig the fly in rhythm. You'll get fish that way, but you'll get more when you watch how the natural swims. A crayfish, he swims in little quick spurts. You've got to hop that thing and pause. Don't get mechanical about it. Hop it two times then pause. Hop it three times then wait for it. That's how you fish a crayfish.

DK: What about your baitfish patterns? Are you fishing those on a sink tip or intermediate line?

CK: I'm a strong believer in a floating line. I've had some mighty good anglers fish with me, and I've been to Michigan, Maine, Canada, Tennessee,

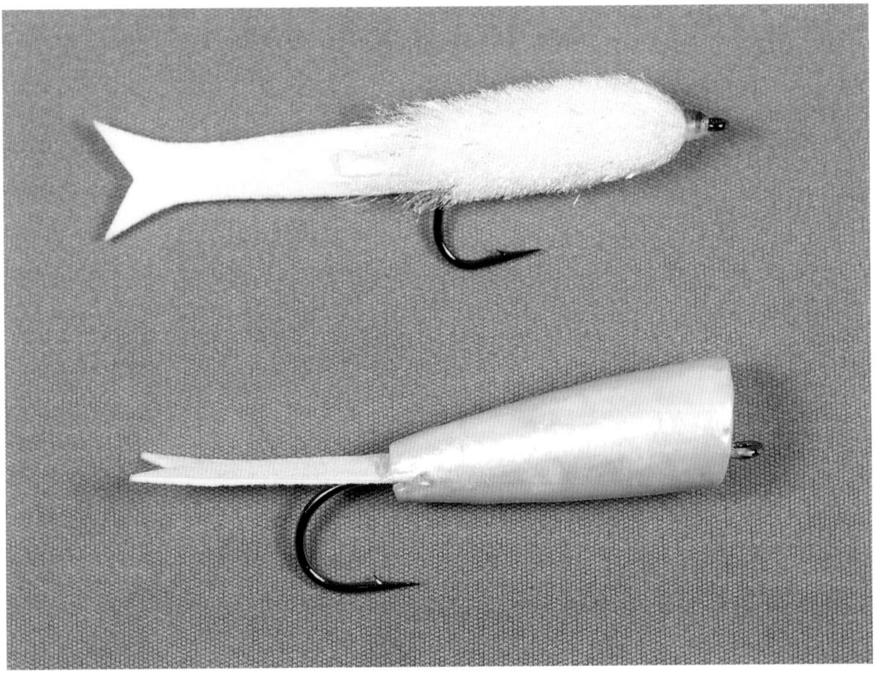

A topwater and a subsurface pattern designed to never lose its profile or silhouette. DAVE KARCZYNSKI

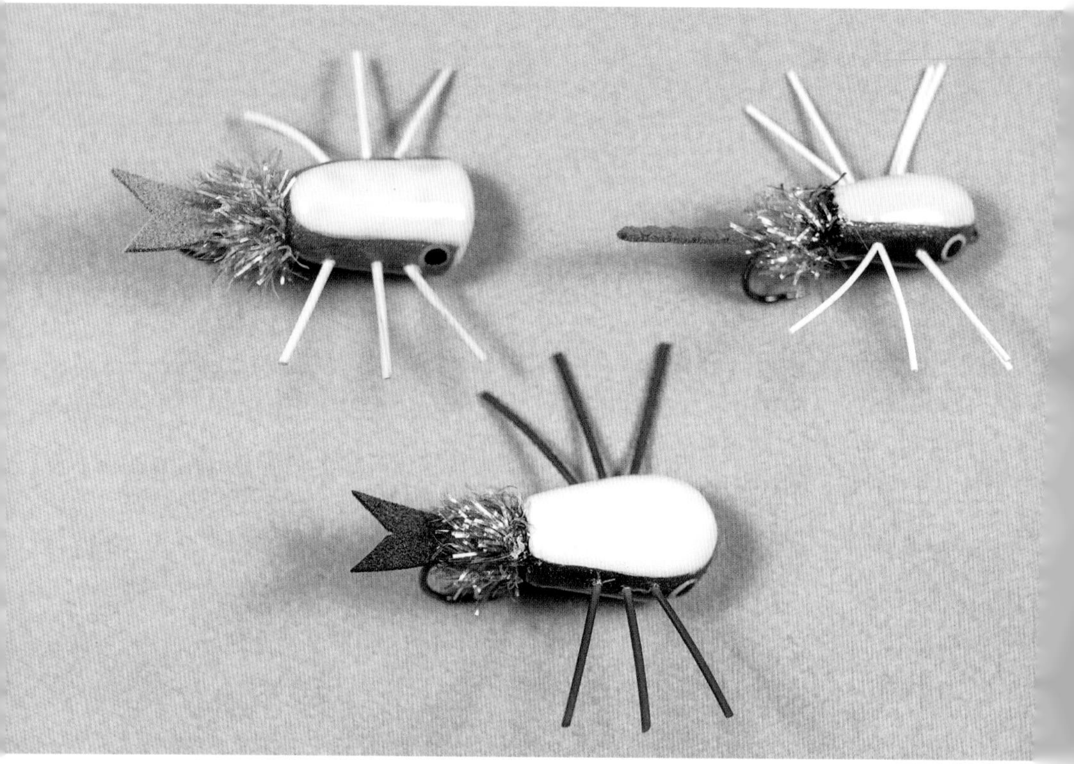

A little flash, a little movement, a little silhouette. These three surface bugs are ready to do whatever's asked of them. DAVE KARCZYNSKI

Arkansas, pretty much everywhere. And I can tell you that my baitfish patterns fish ten times as good on a floating line as with a sinking line.

Same as with the crayfish, if you've got a minnow imitation then you need to make it look like a crippled minnow. And a floating line can really help with that. That's because a floating line always puts an arc on the fly; it's coming through the water but also tilting up to the surface to follow the floating line. And that's just how a crippled or dying baitfish swims. A healthy fish does the opposite: It swims straight in the water. I don't want my flies to swim straight. I want them to tilt up. But of course that doesn't mean you can't fish them lower down in the column. If we need to get deeper we lengthen the leader a bit. So we're fishing down deeper but we're still getting the upward motion on the strip.

DK: How do you approach a given beat of water?

CK: We'll rig up three rods and put a baitfish on one, a Clawdad on another, and a topwater on the third. Between those three you can fish fast and slow, up and down in the column. You've got your bases covered with those three types of flies.

DK: Have you noticed any ways in which big fish behave differently from small fish?

CK: I can only speak to the rivers I fish, but on my rivers the big fish take bugs a little more readily when there's not a lot of movement to them.

DK: What's your best day on the water?

CK: One day Carl Hoffman and I were fishing and we had one of those days when everything was right. By twelve-thirty in the afternoon, he had eight smallmouth over four pounds, and that's not including all the sixteen- to nineteen-inch fish he caught. There were too many sixteen-inch to nineteen-inch fish to count. And three of the big boys were more than five and a half pounds. One might have been six. In any case, around noon Carl is spent and says, "Let's head on in we've had such a good day." But I snapped back at him that I would tell him when it was time to quit. I explained to him you don't get many days like this in your life, and when you do, you keep going. So we kept going. He ended up with ten fish over twenty inches, and God knows how many sixteen- to nineteen-inch fish. That's the thing with smallmouth fishing. Every now and again you get one of those days. They're special no matter how much you fish. You've got to put in as full a day as you can, because you don't know how long it will be till the next one.

Interview: Lefty Kreh on a Lifetime of Smallmouth Fishing

Fly-fishing legend Bernard "Lefty" Kreh has either authored or contributed to more than twenty books over the course of his illustrious fifty-plus-year career. Along the way he revolutionized fly casting, designed various fly rods, and developed legendary fly patterns such as The Deceiver. Lefty received the Lifetime Achievement Award from the American Sportfishing Association and the Lifetime Contribution Award from the American Fly Tackle Trade Association, and he has been inducted into the Freshwater Fishing Hall of Fame as well as the International Game Fish Association Hall of Fame. He lives in Hunt Valley, Maryland.

DK: Legend has it that your first fish on a fly rod was a smallmouth bass. Is that correct?

LK: That's right. It was on the Potomac River. I think it was 1947. It was really the beginning of my fly-fishing career, if you want to call it a career. That first fish came not long after my first casting lesson ever, which just happened to be with Joe Brooks.

DK: How did that come about?

LK: Well, one afternoon I invited Joe fishing. He was just a writer for a small newspaper at the time—he wasn't yet the big deal he'd become later on. I was fishing a baitcasting rod and he was fishing a fly rod on that first outing. And he really impressed me with that fly rod. Nobody I knew in Maryland used a fly rod at that time for bass. They did a bit of trout fishing with a fly rod, but there really was no bass fishing at all with a fly rod. In any case, I was so impressed with how well Joe did on the Potomac with me that the next day I drove fifty miles in a Model-A Ford to where he lived in Baltimore to take a fly-casting lesson from him—and I paid good money for that lesson.

DK: What was that first lesson like?

LK: What he taught me was that nine o'clock to one o'clock stuff that most people teach, which was a good place to start because I had no idea what I was doing with a fly rod. But I knew other tackle. By that time of course I had already caught hundreds of bass on baitcasting tackle. I say baitcasting because this was prior to the spinning reel coming over to the United States from Europe. Of course, there may have been a spinning rod here and there, but for the most part no one knew about them. So prior to taking up the fly rod, I simply threw tiny plugs on a casting reel. And it's because of the reel, or rather, the limitations of the reel that I really got interested in fly casting. That's because over the years of smallmouth fishing I had noticed that smaller lures would catch more fish. The problem was that

Lefty Kreh points out where a bass just rolled on a northern Wisconsin freestoner. NATE SIPPLE

those small lures were hard to cast with the reels we were using. Basically, I needed a different technology to catch more bass.

After I was taught by Joe, I became competent with the nine-to-one style. But it wasn't long before I realized that I just wasn't covering enough water with my casts. I could catch a lot more fish, I knew, if I could add distance and keep my fly on the water longer. This was when I first started to experiment with casting strokes that would really gain the fly angler distance. At the time, nobody took their rod back past two o'clock. It was a religion not to do that. In fact, in 1965 I wrote an article on situational casting in *Outdoor Life* with a drawing that showed how to take the rod back behind you—past two o'clock. Well, they got a lot of nasty letters on the thing. A lot of nasty letters.

DK: What did those first few forays with a fly rod teach you about smallmouth that you hadn't known before?

LK: The first thing I learned was that they sure do take popping bugs! And the second thing it taught me was if I can learn to make longer casts, which I could not do with that limited casting stroke, if I could make longer casts I could catch more fish. And so the smallmouth bass encouraged me, I guess you'd say, to learn a different way of fly casting, which of course over the

One sign of a good popper? It pops every time. MICHAEL LESCHISIN

years would become the way most people cast. So a lot of modern single-handed fly casting can be attributed to the smallmouth and smallmouth bass fishing.

DK: What were the rivers like back then?

LK: They were fantastic. All of our rivers here, the Potomac, the Susquehanna, the Shenandoah, and the James, all these rivers back in the 1940s and 1950s and 1960s were teeming with smallmouth bass. There were just unbelievable amounts of food. Almost all the rocks held hellgramites and crawfish, and you could catch as many madtoms (catfish) for bait as you pleased. All you had to do was take a net down to the grass bed and you could catch ten or fifteen of these madtoms in fifteen, twenty minutes.

Those madtoms were a great bait for bass because you hook them up and they're tougher than a bad mother-in-law. You could use them all day long and at the end of the day they'd still be swimming. So it's true that we had unbelievable smallmouth fishing back then, but plenty has changed in the interim. In fact, you guys living in the North, in Maine and Wisconsin and New England and that area up there, have no idea how pristine your rivers are compared to the rivers we have here now in the Mid-Atlantic region.

Our insect populations have suffered notably as a result. Decades ago the ephorons were so thick that you could barely breathe. I have a photograph from a night I was fishing with Bob Clouser. I had a rigged rod lying on the back deck and it was dark. We were in Bob's boat and he had one of those lights that stick up about three feet when you're running at night. We were just drifting along fishing—this was in the Susquehanna, mind you, below Harrisburg, which is a big city. In any case, there were so many insects around that when I went to look for my fishing outfit that was lying on the back deck, I couldn't find it because it was buried in ephorons. When I picked up the rod I said, "Bob, take a photograph of this." And I put my hand down and held up a pile of ephorons almost the size of a coconut shell. Today, however, you're lucky to see five hundred bugs in an evening. That's the kind of stuff we've lost in a sense.

DK: What's the perfect smallmouth river?

LK: What makes a good smallmouth river is a number of things. First, you got to have little and big bass and stuff to feed both of them. The second thing is, you need cover. In addition to all the nutrients in the water, you need cover. If you're fishing largemouth, wood is often the most important type of habitat. For smallmouth, rocks are terribly important. And not only just rocks: You want different kinds of rocks because different rocks form different kinds of ambush spots for fish of different sizes.

DK: So we should be relieved to catch small fish from time to time?

LK: You bet. You need all your classes to continue to produce good fishing. The best rivers, if you're talking about habitat, the best ones, I think, were in the Mid-Atlantic area. To start with they had a limestone base. That

Don't be disappointed when you catch a small fish. This is just as clear a sign of a healthy smallmouth bass ecosystem as a twenty-one-incher. NATE SIPPLE

limestone leaches minerals, which enriches the water, which enriches the microhabitat, the small insects and things like that.

You also need grass along the shoreline for the minnows to hide in, aquatic grasses for the baby bass to hide in and for the food to hide in. And then you need little riffles and gravel places to aerate the water. You need those highly oxygenated places for your insects to live, and you need slightly bigger rocks for the crawfish. In addition to ripples you need pools where in the wintertime smallmouth have a sanctuary. But a river shouldn't be all long, deep, slow pools. Bass can live there, but there are not nearly as many of them as if there were intermittent pools and ledges and rocks and ripples and so on. You need all these combinations of cover and structure and habitat to feed and provide protection for bass from the time they are fry to the time they are five-pounders.

Lastly, I don't think the perfect smallmouth river should be crystal clear. I firmly believe that when water is too clear it's not good bass fishing. The reason for that is that if you have really clear water the prey can't escape, and so you end up with less food for everyone and therefore smaller bass. If eating is too easy, all the food disappears real quick.

DK: So, smallmouth rivers are all different. What about the fish themselves?

LK: I've never talked to a scientist, but I firmly believe from my own experience, which is more than sixty years of catching bass, that there have got to be several subspecies of smallmouth. We now know that there are fourteen subspecies of bonefish. There are certain places you'll go to and almost never catch a bonefish over three pounds. Other places the bonefish will average three to five pounds. And then there's places where you frequently catch bonefish over ten pounds.

And I wonder if the same is also not true for smallmouth bass. I've been on rivers where you're not going to catch many big bass ever, even if the habitat seems ideal. I'd be curious to hear what the biologists would have to say on the subject.

DK: What advice would you give to the trophy smallmouth bass hunter?

LK: I've been fly fishing and tying flies since the 1950s, and my observations about what takes trophy fish come down to two things: materials and size. Natural materials, be they fur, feathers, or hair, are far more effective on streamers and popping bugs than synthetics. If you're going to use synthetics, you definitely need to incorporate some natural material into them. Straight synthetic flies are not nearly as effective in taking truly large fish, I have found.

The other component of trophy smallmouth flies is size. If you're after big smallmouth, particularly in the spring or fall, then you really need to have flies that are a minimum of four or five inches long. Even longer is better. Some conventional anglers will see my flies and laugh at me. "You're using a seven-inch fly?" And I say, "Well, you're throwing a Rebel plug the same size."

DK: I know you're a fan of fishing topwaters for smallmouth. Describe for us your perfect popping bug.

LK: Well, to do that we need to define the criteria for a good popping bug. First off, a good popping bug is one that's easy to cast but still puts out a good profile in the water. Second, a good popping bug pops every time. Third, it should be easy to lift from the water so you don't scare the fish with that blooping sound when you pick it up. Next, it should hook the fish easily. And finally, it should have rubber legs.

I spent twenty years working on a popping bug that works every time, and you can use it for little tiny brim or you can use it for barracudas. That bug, first of all, uses squirrel tail hair to form the tail of the popper. I'm convinced squirrel hair is superior as a tailing material on popping bugs. If you don't believe me, try this: Tie a fly with any kind of hair except squirrel and tie another one with squirrel tail hair. Then drop them in the water. You'll find that the non-squirrel-hair fibers mat together in the water. Only the squirrel tail hair fibers will flair in every direction. But that's not all. Not only does squirrel give you a larger profile on the water, but when you pick your bug up out of the water to recast, those fibers become as sleek and aerodynamic as can be. Stay away from popping bugs with unnecessary feathers and hackles. They are as pointless as the cute eyeballs and smiley faces that some companies apply.

Lefty's favorite popping bug doesn't waste space and takes no prisoners. DAVE KARCZYNSKI

To get a bug that pops every time, it's all about the shape of the head and the angle of the hook eye. I like a flat face that tapers, and the taper goes from the hook eye up to the top at an angle. That hook eye sits on the bottom of the bug. This makes the bug sit at an angle in the water. With that slanted zing it will make all the noise you want, but when the presentation is over and it's time to pick the fly up, it's already at the right angle to be extracted quietly from the water.

The other thing that you need is a hook longer than the bug body. This will further ensure that the bug sits on the water at an elevated angle, with that face pointing up. Done this way, the hook is the first thing to come into contact with a bass, no matter which angle that bass approaches the bug at. What so many popping bugs do is have the hook positioned almost directly underneath the body, so the fish has to grab the whole body and the hook together to get hooked up.

Last but not least, modern popping bugs need to have legs. But they should be applied in a particular way. Many people make all the bug legs the same size, the result being that the ones in the back tangle in the hook. I leave the legs at the front of the bug long and form a taper moving back toward the tail. The last rubber legs, those closest to the tail, are the shortest—they still twitch but they don't foul the fly, which just makes a wasted cast.

DK: And what about the body? Are you using spun deer hair?

LK: Hell no. Fly fisherman don't fool with no damn deer hair. It's wet and soft and mushy. I want my bugs to float. I usually make them from cork, but I also will use foam when I have to.

DK: Let's move on to the subject of specific fish. What's one fish you wish you could have back?

LK: I was on the Penobscot in Maine, way up near Bangor. The Penobscot is incidentally one of the most unbelievably beautiful smallmouth rivers in the country. It's got grass beds, ledges, everything you need for good smallmouth habitat. As we floated downriver we approached an old mill of some kind, high on a hill with a dam where the water came sluicing out the bottom, making a deep gouge in the river. There were giant swirling eddies and it was quite deep. Luckily I had a lead core line with me, and I put on an eight-inch Deceiver because the guide told me there were some really huge bass in there.

Before I go any further I'm going to tell you that I don't lie about fishing. If you get caught up in a real lie then no one will ever believe you again. So what I'm about to tell you is factually true. I put this Deceiver on and did what I do in extremely deep eddy water, which is count the fly down and let the fly swirl about in the current. This fly sank eight or ten feet and then I felt something and I set the hook. Well, out of the

Oftentimes it's the fish we don't catch that stay with us the longest. Any angler who has pursued the smallmouth with dedication has lost a good fish that went airborne at the wrong moment.

LUKE KAVAJECZ

water came a smallmouth that went well, well over seven pounds. It was at least twenty-eight or twenty-nine inches long, just an unbelievable fish. I fought that darn thing for probably five minutes. It jumped several times. But apparently the hook set I put on it in that swirling water didn't really amount to much, because I lost it. That was definitely the best smallmouth that I ever hooked and lost.

The other place I know of where there are definitely six- and seven-pound river smallmouths is the New River below Claytor Lake. The problem is that much of that water is not only very clear but very deep. In seven and eight feet of water, you can still easily see the bottom. And the river gets much deeper than that. The problem is that it's extremely difficult to get flies down to them in clear water with a fly line. But if you can find a way, you can get into some truly large fish. Chuck Craft was the top guy down there for years. He showed me records and photos of fish six and seven pounds that some of his clients caught. There are some big fish there, but that one on the Penobscot that day was bigger. And that's no lie.

DK: Leave us with your favorite smallmouth memory.

LK: Probably the most memorable bass I ever caught happened when I was wading in the Potomac above Brunswick, Maryland, which is about forty miles above Washington, DC. I was using that Lefty's bug I just described.

Anyways, while wading in shallow water and casting the bug into four foot of water, I caught my first five-pound smallmouth. Actually he weighed five pounds, four ounces exactly. I shouldn't have done it, but I brought it home, I was so damned tickled with him.

DK: Is that fish on the wall now?

LK: No, I never mounted it. I just came home and like a young kid, I probably was only in my twenties, I had to show it to everybody. It wasn't so easy to share images of fish back in the day. Most of us never had a camera. It was definitely a different time.

Interview: Larry Dahlberg on Migratory Fish, Jumping to Conclusions, and the Birth of the Diver

Minnesotan Larry Dahlberg has been fishing the rivers of the Upper Mississippi watershed for decades. After guiding for twenty-three years, he turned to educating anglers on how to catch fish and make their own flies and lures. Larry is the recipient of the Henshall Award for the promotion of warm-water fly fishing, as well as the IGFA Conservation Award. His many fish-catching inventions include Flashabou, the Dahlberg Diver, and the Whopper Plopper. He currently designs lures for River2Sea. You can find him online at huntforbigfish.com and makelure.com.

DK: When did you start following the movements of smallmouth bass through your river systems?

LD: It was in an attempt to promote catch-and-release regulations in areas where smallmouth congregated during the cold-water months and were vulnerable. A lot of anglers who were opposed to the regulations argued that smallmouth never left their home lies. We found that to be untrue. We tagged many, many, many, many fish, and during that first year of following them we found a significant number of fish as far as eighty miles from where they were tagged. I have documentation of these bronze fish moving eighty miles in a period of a couple of weeks.

DK: When does that happen?

LD: When the water hits sixty degrees in the fall, they start sliding downhill. Interestingly, when I lived on the Mississippi in Brainerd, the fish went the opposite direction. They wintered upstream below the power dam in Brainerd on the Mississippi.

DK: So they know where that deep water is, then?

Larry Dahlberg takes bass whenever, wherever, and however he can, whether that be via an original lure or one of the fly designs. LARRY DAHLBERG

LD: Apparently. But confirming that they traveled a great distance wasn't the only shocking thing I learned from those early tagging studies. Even wilder is how specific these fish were in their annual relocations. I had fish that I tagged on spawning beds that then went away for the summer, moved down to the reservoir for the winter, and then came back to the same spot to spawn the next year. And we're not talking general vicinity. I'm talking about catching fish from the exact same rock that they were hanging out beside the year before.

DK: Wow, so even a little bit territorial.

LD: No little bit about it. They act like warm-water salmon, which is just fascinating. An angler might say, "Well, what does that migratory nature mean to me?" What that means is that if you know your water really well, and you recognize that there are certain periods of the year where bass have to swim through areas that don't offer a whole lot of cover, during those periods an angler who knows the neighborhood can really, really have some fun fishing.

DK: So we're talking now about transitional water that they're passing through en route to their wintering grounds.

LD: Yes, only I wouldn't call it "transitional water." I'd call it "places with less cover." It's typically big, wide, flat, shallow water with a minimum of holding pools. There might be a logjam somewhere in the middle of a sand run. In three feet of water there could be three-, four-, five-pounders sitting on the stupid thing. When I first saw them I was like, what the hell are they doing here? And now I know it's just a pit stop on their travels. They're going along and all of a sudden they say, "Hey, here's a Seven Eleven. I'll hang out for a minute."

We discovered this tendency a bit by accident. I was fishing with the best fly fisherman I was ever in a boat with, a man named Chuck Walton, the head chemist at 3M. He was the guy that made the decision, I think, to go into tapes and adhesives. He held a world record for permit for a long, long time, and he was a phenomenal angler and great caster. The first time he came smallmouth fishing, he was with one of the other guides, and the guide was rowing like hell through a bunch of wood out in the middle of the river, trying to blow through the dead water and get to the next spot. Walton always wanted to cast, so he was going to do it from a fast-moving boat if he had to. So he puts on a Lefty's Deceiver and starts throwing ninety footers out into the river, slightly ahead of the boat so he's not skipping his fly, and he catches a six-pounder.

DK: That's a huge fish. Have you noticed a difference between the behavior of those extra large fish, four or five pounds, as compared to smaller fish? Are there any fundamental differences?

LD: Yeah. Yeah, they take the best place in the area. They always occupy the best spot. Prime-lie oriented. If their populations haven't had the shit kicked out of them, they usually kind of hang together as a year class. Smallmouth are very year-class oriented. Even when they migrate—that's when their year-class clumping behavior is most interesting, I think. I see the larger fish first, though I don't know why. I've never figured it out. It's not by several weeks, but by maybe a week.

DK: In other interviews you've given, you talk a lot about not rushing to conclusions when theorizing fish behavior. Can you speak more on why you don't like to rush to conclusions?

LD: I don't rush because it's really, really easy to come to the wrong conclusions, especially if you're fly fishing exclusively. If you're fly fishing, the only conclusion that you can come to—and I say this with the greatest respect to fly anglers—is on those occasions when you can actually see the fish, right there on the bottom. If you can see the fish against the bottom and you present and he didn't bite, you can be certain there was a fish there that didn't bite. Otherwise the only reality check, the only way you can come to conclusions with certainty, is with live bait. Live bait is just a different thing. I can take you to smallmouth places, and I don't care how good you are

There's no substitute for time on the water when it comes to dialing in the biggest of big fish on your watershed. LARRY DAHLBERG

with a fly rod or what you can tie or buy or whatever, you'll say there are no fish here. Then I'll get out some live bait and catch twenty or thirty fish, and you'll say "Holy shit." What I'm trying to say is you just can't come to conclusions with a fly. Flies are just invalid when it comes to fish behavior theory. You can never come to any meaningful conclusion unless you've got the option of live bait.

And even with bait there's the problem of not being everywhere at once. That makes it difficult to reach conclusions as well. How can you say with confidence, "The fish aren't biting," if you're on a river with a hundred navigable fishable miles and you've only touched three of them? You can't. When I was a kid, I used to take a boat and float ten, twelve, fifteen miles and then camp. Now I've got a jet that runs fifty miles an hour and I'll run sixty, seventy miles in a day just so I can confirm or disconfirm a suspicion about what fish are up to. And I've really learned a lot as a result of that. One thing is their position. Once they've established themselves in the summer, smallmouth don't move too much. There's really only two movements. I've found them when they come up out of the reservoir in the spring. I've caught them on the way up in the same places as I catch them on the way down. Those are the limited cover areas I was referring to.

DK: What advice would you give to the young kid growing up who wants to be the next Larry Dahlberg?

LD: I'd say you've got to watch everything. I learned a lot, almost everything, from watching. As a kid, my old man used to drop me off in the swamp and I'd go catch crayfish below the dam, fill a bucket, and have quite a bit of live bait. Then I'd head out to the river, climb trees that leaned out over the channel, and drop crayfish one by one into the flow. I'd watch how the crayfish moved and the smallmouth reacted. I did the same thing with worms—really with whatever I could get my hands on. I harassed these smallmouth bass in a way an adult would never do, just experimenting. And I learned really a lot that way. And once I started guiding I kept watching, kept observing, kept making notes. All that watching has made the difference.

DK: What's one unusual trait you've observed?

LD: Here's an interesting characteristic. You could take an aquarium, six by six, four by four, twelve feet by twelve feet, doesn't matter. It could be made of glass, cement, whatever you want. Put two smallmouth and two largemouth into the aquarium and at the end of three days, you'll see the largemouth all have bruises on their bottom lips where the skin has torn away because they're all banging into walls. But the smallmouth won't have any at all.

DK: Let's finish up with you telling us the story of the Dahlberg Diver.

LD: Okay. There I am, a young guide guiding these people that are all millionaires and stuff. To a kid like me of course they're just a bunch of

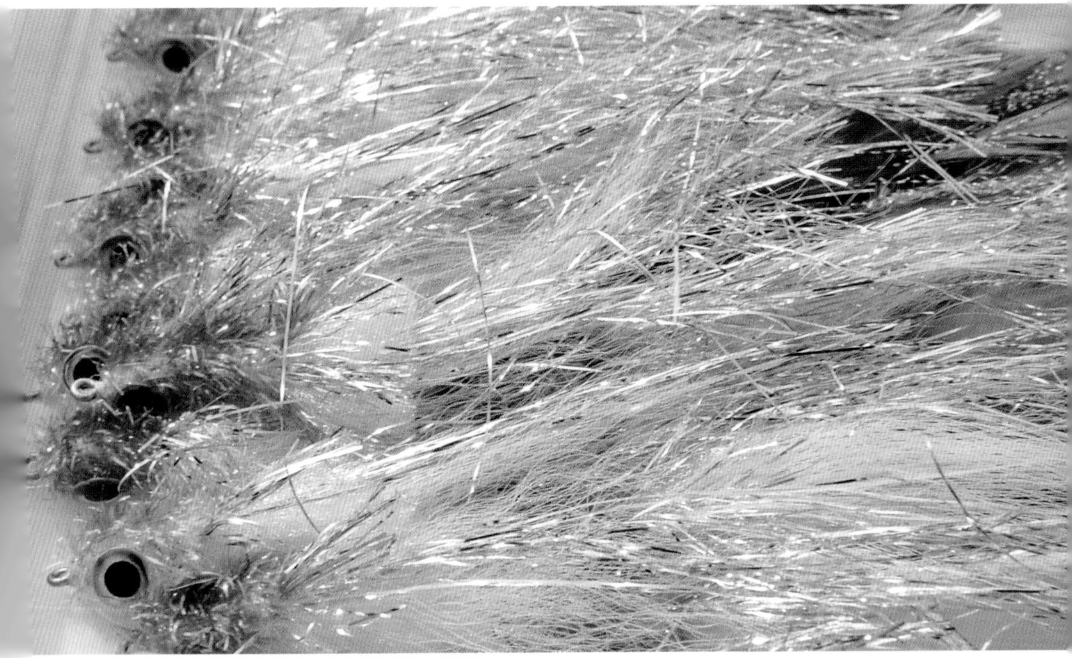

Dahlberg's development of Flashabou ushered in a new era of flies and fly tying. NATE SIPPLE

incompetent city people. Otherwise, why would they need me? Among them is a man named Tom Daniels who was one of the founders of the ADM company—Archer Daniels Midland. It was this big, giant, monster company. In any case, Tom Daniels is one of the founders. He would come up every year smallmouth fishing with his wife and we'd go out in a couple of boats. His wife, June, who was a very sweet lady, always wanted to fish with me. Only Tom and June had a bet each time they went out, a three-dollar. There was one dollar for the first fish, one dollar for the biggest fish, and one dollar for the most fish. Well, when I met Mrs. Daniels, she'd never caught a smallmouth in her life. She'd been coming up to this camp for a long time, and every time she went out, she'd end up paying her husband three dollars. And she always insisted on fishing with me. It drove me nuts; I didn't think it was fair. Anyhow, I'm thinking what to put on Mrs. Daniel's line that will get her a fish. I want to put on a spinner, but I can't because she's either hung up all the time or hitting one of us in the head because she can't cast fifteen feet.

Anyhow, one year I look at my guide calendar and see the Daniels are coming up, so I start trying to figure out some way that I could make something that Mrs. Daniels could catch a fish on. And I caught a glimpse of some Mylar tinsel in my fly-tying kit and it gave me an idea. How did that tinsel get there in the first place? I'll tell you. I grew up real poor. My mom was real cheap. At Christmas she bought this stuff at the store that was the cheapest Christmas tree tinsel that money could by. Mylar had just been invented, and this was Mylar tinsel. I was reaching up to put a piece of it on the top limb of the Christmas tree and I missed the branch and the tinsel fluttered slowly to the ground. I looked at that fluttering and I thought "That's a spinner." So after the holidays were over I collected all that cheap tinsel and put it in my fly tying kit.

So before that Daniels trip in question, I took a hunk of tinsel and tied it to the hook shank. Then I remembered that Mrs. Daniels often fell asleep at the switch, so I needed to make sure it didn't sink. So I took a piece of cork about the diameter of a pencil and used it for the body, then spun a little muddler-type piece of deer-hair head in front of that. I had no idea if it would work, but I stuck it in my fly box.

Mrs. Daniels shows up and we jump in my boat. Her husband goes off with another guide in the opposite direction. We go to this place where I knew there would be a whole bunch of little ones. I had her throw the tinsel and cork contraption out there and we started swinging it back and forth in the current. It was shining and wiggling in the current, and I thought, "That's a pretty good imitation of a Mepps spinner." Well wouldn't you know it, Mrs. Daniels catches her first smallmouth ever, and her second, and her third, and her fourth, and fifth. Then we were kind of losing count, so she started tearing the heads off of matches. She had a book of matches with her, being a fairly heavy smoker. Each time she caught a fish, she'd tear a match head off. When she ran out of match heads, she started making little tears in the matchbook. Anyway, we caught all sorts of fish, and after the matchbook was headless and torn every which way, she suddenly decided she wanted a cigarette. Only I didn't have any matches and she didn't either. So we hopped it down to the lunch spot and waited for the rest of the group to come, and they showed up with matches. She had a cigarette, and that day she won all three dollars. She didn't always win three dollars after that. Usually she didn't catch the biggest, but she always caught the first and the most. I made sure of that. And it was all on account of this flashy material. Later I showed it to some guy who was in the business and then he and I refined it and used some different, superior materials. Then I copyrighted the name. Today it's called Flashabou.

Interview: Mike Schultz and the Cold-Water Frontier

Mike Schultz (known as "Schultzy" to most) is the owner of Schultz Outfitters Fly Shop & Guide Service, which specializes in southeastern Michigan angling, instruction, and destination travel (schultzoutfitters.com). Born and raised in the great state of Michigan, Schultzy has been immersed in the outdoors his entire life. After graduating from Eastern Michigan University with a Bachelor of Business Administration, he started guiding and working in the fly-fishing industry full-time.

Logging countless hours on the water each year, Schultzy has developed a vast knowledge of Midwestern waters and beyond. The bulk of his guiding and angling takes place on his home waters of southeastern Michigan; these rivers offer world-class warm-water fishing. His angling travels have taken him from Patagonia to Russia and many places in between.

Over the years, with the help of the Huron River Watershed Council, he founded the Huron River Single Fly tournament as well as Huckin for the Huron. Both are annual fund-raisers that take place on his home waters of the Huron River, Michigan's Blue Ribbon smallmouth stream. During the spring of 2014 Schultzy was honored with the HRWC Partner of the Year award.

Schultzy is a member of the Simms Fishing Products ELITE and YETI Ambassador programs and is on the pro staff at Scientific Anglers, Costa Del Mar, Clackacraft, and Regal Vises. His signature fly patterns are available through Fulling Mill (fullingmill.com). He currently resides in Dexter, Michigan, on the banks of the Huron River with his wife, Allie, and sons, Tanner and Dylan.

DK: I know you've always fished and guided Michigan smallmouth bass in the month of April, but this was the first year that your home waters were open 365 days a year for catch-and-release smallmouth fishing. What did you learn while fishing in February and March?

MS: We learned a lot because we started fishing much, much, much earlier. It being a mild winter in Michigan, the first fishable weather of the year came in February. We had a spell of sixty-degree weather in the middle of February. The first fish that we heard about being caught last year on the fly was right around Valentine's Day. February twenty-third was the first day I went out personally. I spent the whole day before browsing online, trying to find information about cold-weather smallmouth. If you google "cold-weather smallmouth fishing" you get a bunch of hits from Alabama, Tennessee, places like that. Being from Michigan my thinking was: "What's cold to you guys?" I also noticed that a lot of the information that you could find had to do with lakes, and even that information dealt

After several decades on the water, Mike Schultz has the biggest bass of southeast Michigan on speed dial. COREY HASELHUHN

with forty-plus-degree water temps, whereas we were dealing with water temps just above freezing.

So on the twenty-third it was a mild winter day with fifty-degree air temps, but as I mentioned we still had thirty-four-degree water temps. Even so, it didn't take us long to get into fish, which shocked all of us. We fished this stretch of river where you've got all these whoops and dips going down through it, like a gravel run. And I was just like, "Let's just drop anchor and let's just swing some flies." So I fished a weighted Feather Game Changer that I had tied. Cold weather means natural colors, or so I thought at the time, so I had a few Game Changers in natural colors, tan grizzly, the whole thing, with a big heavy bead in addition to the lead wraps to get it down. One big thing I learned from my first winter smallmouth season ever in southern Michigan is that your go-to summer smallmouth lines fish like old-school telephone cord. But we fought through it. Within five minutes of swinging through that wobbly water, I got a twelve-incher. As I released it I was like, "Hmm, thirty-four-degree water temps and we already got a fish. This cold-water bassing thing just might happen."

After that fish I got in the rower's seat and my buddy started casting. All of a sudden he yells, "Did you see that? I swear a fish just came off that log." Strip, strip, strip, strip, "There he is!" The fish he hooked up with had moved twenty-five feet to eat that leech. We were just like, "Huh? What? A smallmouth moving twenty-five feet for a fly in thirty-four-degree water in February?" You think you'd want to fish a jig fly right on its nose. But no. This fish just swam off a log across the sandbar into the main current of the river and ate the fly right off his rod tip. And these February fish were busting at the gut, too, just wide fish. We were like, when did you start feeding? Yesterday? Last week?

DK: That is absolutely insane.

MS: We felt the same way. After we released that fish we were like, what's going on here? I think we ended up catching maybe a half dozen that day. It wasn't lights out or anything, and there was definitely a window. I think we put in at like eleven o'clock and we caught all our fish between noon and three o'clock. But it was so unique.

DK: What else did you guys learn as the season unfolded?

MS: A lot. After we caught that fish in February, we fished again right away and just kept fishing and just gathered a bunch of data. During that time we went to three or four different rivers. On some of the rivers, the parks weren't even open yet, so it was kind of weird. But the surprising thing is the big fish that we catch multiple times over the course of any given year were in the same exact spot as they are in the summer. Well, not the same exact spot; let's just call it a hole. In the summertime they might be in a different lie, but those big fish were there in the same vicinity. The water was lower than average this year—it was crystal clear—so we could float over to those spots and go, "There he is, there's him, and him, and her." Of course, smallmouth migration is different on every river, and this particular river has a lot of dams, which limits fish movement.

In any case, we fished a lot during late February and early March. And the days were pretty similar. We'd be floating down not seeing much, and then we would get into some activity. One day we fished for three or four hours and didn't touch a fish. Like, nothing. Didn't move a fish, didn't see a fish. Then we came to this water I had mentally prepared to really pound, a super deep pool, a perfect pool, the kind of place you look at in the summer and think, "This is where they're going to live in the winter."

We get in there, Carson's on the bow, I'm rowing, James is in the back. First Carson hooks up, nineteen and three-quarters, just a fricking tank, an awesome fish. We take a picture of it, row to the bank, get some photos, throw it back out. James hits a seventeen. Carson drops anchor, lets the fish go, puts a line out, boom: eighteen. I'm in the back, I'm like, "To heck with you guys." We went over the hole again and got another another, which made it four in one spot. We ended with seven fish out of that pool, with

As Tanner Schultz aptly demonstrates, you're never too young to get your bass on. COREY HASELHUHN

the biggest being twenty and seven-eighths inches, after not touching a fish for the first four miles of water.

DK: What do you attribute that activity to?

MS: It was location obviously, because there was a bunch of fish concentrated there, but it was also the bite window. It was during that middle of the day, the warmest time, even though it was just above freezing and raining sideways. It was the right water, too. For these cold-water smallmouth you want the laziest water, which makes a lot of sense because in the winter there's higher oxygen levels in the dead water than there is in the fast water—it's the opposite of what you would think of in the summer as oxygenated water.

DK: Interesting.

MS: The first person to tell me about that oxygen phenomenon was Kevin Feenstra. He always used to talk about super cold-weather trout fishing on the Muskegon and fishing in pretty much frog water and catching tons of trout. It has to do with how cold it is. What we'd find that time of year was the same thing; the bass would be in these dead couch water areas, usually on structure, usually on wood. Like I said, every river's different, but I use this river a lot as an example because I think it's one of the most difficult rivers to fish. What makes it difficult is, first off, the amount of people that enjoy it, whether it be from a kayak or with a baitfishing rod or whatever. But secondly, we just don't have the numbers of fish like you have in the Saginaw River tributaries, where you've got just massive influxes of bait that bass just eat all year long. You can sustain a lot of bass in certain tributaries.

In any case, the one thing all our spots had in common was depth and proper speed. I always call it smallmouth speed. It's not super fast, it's not super slow, it's just kind of perfect. Early in the season we were finding these fish and they weren't obviously on the main currents—they were in the softer water—but they had to have some current nearby, just like you see on any of the rivers that we all know. If you find the current, you find the fish. If you don't have current, forget it. Even though they're sitting in water that doesn't have current—say, a table-size area of dead water—the current's right there just a few feet away from the fish. They're always going to have something to bring them food.

DK: How did these fish act differently from warm-water fish?

MS: We noticed during all those first three floats that the fish that we did see move on the fly, it was almost like they were drunk. They were just real lethargic, and a couple fish missed the fly. The fish were almost moving in slow motion. We attribute that to water temps.

DK: Let's talk a little bit more about the flies you were throwing. I'm presuming you started out with your classic dumbbell flies.

MS: Yeah, red-eyed leeches, sculpin patterns, just natural stuff. I wouldn't say to a smallmouth angler, "You've got to have this color flash or this color thing," but I think one thing for the smallmouth angler to look at is what the gear guys are doing. The gear guy doesn't just have one size jig, or one weight jig. He's got six different weights of jigs in different sizes. And that's a key to the smallmouth fly angler, too, especially the cold-water smallmouth angler. In the spring we were using medium dumbbell eyes, large dumbbell eyes, extra large dumbbell eyes, and sometimes even extra large dumbbells with a tungsten bead on top. We had flies in all different sizes, too. We kept experimenting with size and weight until we found what the fish wanted to eat on a given day.

DK: I'm imagining these fly patterns had lots of passive action, plenty of rabbit, marabou, rubber legs, all that good stuff that works so well in cold water.

MS: Right, but we didn't stay with those flies too long. We're always looking to push the limits, so after a few weeks of fishing we began wondering, "Let's see what we can do with swim flies." And not naturally colored swim flies either but bright white swim flies. I like to fish white whenever possible. If I get to see the fly get eaten, even though the rod's in the client's hands, that's what I want to see. If I can get one strike on white and three strikes on black but I can't see that black fly getting eaten, I'll just use the white. White seems to work everywhere that I've fished it, and it's fun to fish.

Swim flies like the Swingin' D move water with their foam heads and swerve in enticing erratic ways with their many articulated shanks. COREY HASELHUHN

DK: So it's cold water, early April in Michigan, and you're throwing white swim flies, not dark colored dredgers or deep strippers but bright white swim flies.

MS: You got it. I hadn't yet developed the Deep D, so we just had the original Swingin' D and the Mini D, which I didn't think would get down deep enough. So we went with white Feather Game Changers. I started fishing those in white on April second with a killer angler, one of the best anglers I've ever had the privilege of guiding. We go out to a known lie and I'm like, "All right, there's a fish up here that I see all the time in the summer; it's gigantic. It's on the left-hand side. I don't know where he's going to be today because I've never been up here this time of year. Let's find him."

My client makes one cast, two casts, three casts, whatever, and then suddenly it's fish on. "Damn," I'm thinking. "He's got The One." Then this gigantic submarine of a bass comes to the surface, rolls around, and the fly comes unbuttoned. I'm just quiet, devastated. If it was summer, I would have jumped out of the boat to go get that fish. It was that big. My client goes, "Don't worry, we'll get another one." And I'm thinking, "Another one? It's snowing sideways, it's thirty degrees outside, the water temp is like thirty-six, and you're confident that you're going to get another chance at a huge smallmouth?" Sure enough, he did get another great one, a twenty-and-three-quarter-inch fish I'd last seen on October seventh of the previous year. Then we got into some largemouth, which I thought was really strange. I think we probably got maybe ten fish that day, mostly smallmouth, some pike, largemouth, and a walleye mixed in. Not bad when there's snow in your face and you're throwing a white swim fly. The other strange thing about these particular bass is that they were in two, three, four feet of water. It wasn't like you were finding them in the deepest of deep holes.

DK: What do cold-water takes feel like?

MS: They definitely aren't the devastating eats you have in the summer. It's just a subtle pickup: "I'm snagged on the bottom. Oh, the snag's moving." That kind of scenario.

DK: Are you modifying the amount of flash at all on early season flies?

MS: Just the opposite, actually. Early season fish are much less spooky on my water than summer fish. Part of that is how heavily trafficked our rivers are with kayakers, tubers, all kinds of things, once the summer arrived. So in the summer on the technical water, I don't use much flash at all. But in the early season you've got the place to yourself, no one's messing with it, and we've found that bass are less discriminating when it comes to flash. They were eating flashy stuff, they were eating straight white, they were eating leeches and whatnot.

DK: What tips would you give anglers looking to fish your latest swim flies in the cold water, since with the Deep D there's now a fly for every time of year?

MS: The Swingin' D family has got to be fished where the current is pushing on that head, pulling this thing against the current. One of the things we tell clients fishing these flies is that you're not so much stripping the fly back to you as you are letting the boat do some of the work. You want the guy on the sticks to control the boat so it's falling back into the fish. You're keeping the line taut and that thing's wiggling and it's just falling back into fishy lies, kind of like plugging on a steelhead trip. That's the best way to get whacked. It's definitely not trout fishing. That's the biggest thing that I could tell anybody, not only with my flies but with any smallmouth fly. It doesn't matter if you're leeching, you're dredging sculpins, fishing these swim flies, whatever. You always want a forty-five-degree angle or greater downstream when approaching from a boat or even on foot. You're bringing that fly in against the current and at the same time letting it fall back into the fish.

DK: Talk to us about line and leader setups.

MS: It's really a case-by-case basis, given your river's depth, size, and flows. But the one line that stays in the boat, it doesn't matter if it's March, July, or November, is an intermediate. You've just got to have an intermediate line in the boat. They cast easy, sink well; you can obviously tweak the weight of your flies and the length of your leader to get to your desired depth.

This long, post-spawn fish was ready to put the feedbag on and regain some lost weight.

COREY HASELHUHN

They're just so versatile. Even if you're not the world's greatest caster, you're going to be able to get it out to thirty feet with a little bit of coaching.

As for tippet, I never fish anything less than sixteen pound. Even in cold, clear water, I don't downsize. The leader formula is pretty simple: equal lengths of #30-#25- #20/#16 or a #25-#20-#16. We often fish fairly short leaders in the three-foot range, but you can lengthen them to fish deeper—just keep the proportions equal.

DK: What's your strategy for when you do get to the spot you want to soak?

MS: We call it running laps, and we've found good success with it. But first you need to find the right spot to fish. Don't waste your time fishing everything when the water's cold. You've really got to get to the point where you can identify that productive water. The days are still pretty short in the early season, so you're not able to put in ten-hour days like we like to do in the summer. You'll waste a lot of time if you don't pay attention to what's going on, so either using a motor or just manning up and rowing your butt off to get to those good spots is what you want to do.

Once you find that hole, start running laps. For us, this means you fish a hole, row back up, have a beer, have a snack, whatever, and then go through it again. It's usually like a three-two-one scenario, by which I mean you're going to catch three fish on the first lap, two on the second, one or none on the third—at which point it's time to move on downstream. Sometimes after fish have gotten smart to the boat, we'll get out of the boat and fish from the bank. It sounds like a lot of work, but when fish are stacked up, you need to get on them when you can.

DK: Let's talk about that other cold-water season: late fall. It sounds like it's a different game.

MS: I think the first thing we could probably throw out there is that cold-water smallmouth bass fishing is really a case-by-case basis. No two watersheds are identical. Where I guide in southeast Michigan, the Huron is different from the Shiawassee, which is different from the Flint, which is different from the Raisin, which is different from the Grand. And a lot of those differences in how fish feed in cold water have to do with food source. So "What are they eating?" becomes the operative question. Take a river like the Huron, which has dams on top of dams as it flows toward Lake Erie. All those dams mean you don't get a big influx of baitfish like you do on some of the other rivers that come out of say, Lake Huron or Lake Michigan or Lake Erie. So while some rivers have good early-season fishing, others—those baitfish rivers—have good late-season fishing.

The Saginaw watershed is an example of a river that can fish well late into the season. The rivers that flow into Saginaw Bay get a big influx of bait. There are some days when you can't find an inch of water without shad in it. Shad on top of shad on top of shad, like millions of shad. On that particular river, the latest I've ever run a guide trip was December

The last fish of the day returns to an underwater world that only it fully understands. One day, he'll be caught again. DAVE KARCZYNSKI

third. We went up there and we had a seventeen-fish day, and most of the fish were sight fish. I would just stand on the cooler and say, "Oh, there's one," and the fish was sitting in the sun out on a sandbar in like two feet of water. You'd put a minnow on those things and they'd swim ten feet to get it. That's what a big influx of fall baitfish gets you: smallmouth bass that are still feeding, still looking to play ball, even as winter approaches. Meanwhile, on my home river, the Huron, which as I mentioned is stuck between dams with no big influx of bait, there was absolutely no fishing to be had at all. Those fish turn off a lot earlier.

DK: One of the things that makes fish interesting is the mystery. Leave us with a mystery, something that keeps you up at night, thinking and plotting.

MS: Last year in September we were fishing on a day when the water was just too calm and clear to get anything to eat. But we could see probably better than any September day ever before. And there were just all these fish that I'd never seen before. We counted I think forty-eight fish that we figured were eighteen inches or bigger. One logjam had twelve fish like that on it. And I was thinking, "Where did you all come from, and why are you here, all of a sudden?" It was just one of those beautiful days, bright sun, no chop on the water. Of course, we didn't catch any fish because they saw us coming a mile away. Still, it was just amazing how many fish were in there, more than I'd ever seen on water I'd been fishing for decades. Then we went in there and did that same float again in the middle of October and saw only one fish for two miles. It was weird. Very weird. When it comes to smallmouth bass fishing, there are always questions.

Index

Note: Page numbers followed by suffix "p" indicate photos or photo captions (e.g. 84p).